Lynne Falkin McClure, PhD

Risky Business: Managing Employee Violence in the Workplace

Pre-publication
REVIEWS,
COMMENTARIES,
EVALUATIONS . . .

"**T**his book definitely raised my awareness level for potentially dangerous behaviors in the workplace. McClure provides helpful guidelines and examples for the manager to recognize behaviors that may lead to violence–and what to do about them.

Today, we can no longer afford to gloss over inappropriate behaviors as "normal" for the individual. You think you know your co-workers well enough, but after reading this, you may think again. Every manager will appreciate the "what you *must* and *must not do* chapter when employees behave in high-risk ways."

Wayne E. Reisenauer, MBA
Vice President of Land Development,
Northwest Building Corporation

"A casual reader of McClure's work may view the cases cited as rather routine–similar to situations faced daily by all managers. The remarkable contribution of this book is to demonstrate that these rather routine situations are symptoms of potential violence which could have devastating effects on workers, family members, and customers. Recognizing these symptoms, and understanding how to deal with them and how to prevent them from becoming dangerous to other workers is a new discipline that is now required for managers. By identifying and codifying dangerous behavior, McClure legitimizes the discomfort long felt by workers and managers, and increases the potential that unacceptable behavior can be acted upon before it erupts into violence.

McClure's treatment of the relationship between stress and violent behavior is essential for managers to understand. The principles in the book may enable a manager to respond to certain behaviors in a positive, helpful way, instead of waiting until a violent incident must be dealt with. The author makes a strong case that violence in the workplace can result from poor employee performance and poor management. This book contains good suggestions that can lead to good management practices, whether or not prevention of violence is the objective prompting their application."

Alan J. Doman, MBA, CPA
Senior Vice President,
Washington Mutual Bank,
Seattle, Washington

"R *isky Business* provides an in-depth review of potential negative employee behavior in the workplace. Well written and particularly enlightening, it provides useful insight to a missing piece of the puzzle, is easy to read, and may quickly be regarded as a must-read how-to manual for line supervisors and managers."

Jerry M. Brockey, PhD
Executive Vice Chancellor,
Seattle Community College District,
Seattle, Washington

"**R**isky Business examines the growing threat of violence in the workplace. As the book points out, for women, the number one cause of occupational death is homicide; for men, homicide is second only to vehicle accidents. Yet, unlike the news media that sensationalize violent attacks and then dismiss them as random, *Risky Business* defines the behavior patterns every supervisor and manager should be trained to spot. This book tells bosses what they must and must not do when employees become a potential risk. Then it warns all who care how they may be unintentionally encouraging violence at work.

If you have ever puzzled over quirky behavior at work, whether by a colleague or subordinate, read this book. In it, McClure not only solves the puzzle of workplace violence, she has done it in a highly readable, informative style."

William B. Werther, Jr., PhD
Friedland Professor
of Executive Management,
University of Miami,
Coral Gables, Florida

"**W**hether we like it or not, human tragedy is part of life, and our workplace is not exempt. Lynne McClure's *Risky Business* brings this unrecognized risk out in the open and tells us how to deal with it. No supervisor's skill tool box is complete without knowing how to detect problem behaviors and how to do something about them.

On a broader scale, McClure's book is encyclopedic in its description of undesirable behavior at work. This behavior costs businesses and workers much more than just the risk of a violent act. One individual's negative behavior, if not corrected, can destroy the most precious company asset: goodwill. Thank God McClure admonishes us to address this behavior with antidotes that we should all be familiar with: courage, reason, and proactive enlightened business practices."

Ed Bachrach, BS
Chairman and President,
Bachrach Mens Fashions

"**F**or managers who are knowledgable about violent behaviors at work, this book serves as a valuable resource in identifying high-risk employees and offers a practical nuts and bolts approach to what to do about it. Managers who have not considered the consequences of violent behavior for their organization and employees should regard this book as must reading. For employees of either large or small corporations, *Risky Business* is a training guide for how to make the workplace safer by defining the healthy workplace environment.

The seep of violence into the workplace has affected millions of Americans. Tragically, the fear generated from these acts has severely affected morale in the workplace and is fast approaching a national crisis. This timely book addresses these concerns in a straightforward manner that allows managers to identify high-risk employees while offering many pragmatic suggestions on how to intervene. McClure also includes many stimulating vignettes that enhance the presentation. Of particular benefit to managers will be the chapters dealing with preventative remedies for high-risk behaviors that can be instituted throughout companies. These remedies can function as a safety net that prevents problems from escalating into tragedies.

McClure has provided a real service to managers with this book. It is destined to increase productivity in the workplace and most of all to save lives."

Neil Weiner, PhD
Psychologist and Adjunct Professor, Mesa, Arizona

The Haworth Press, Inc.

Risky Business
Managing Employee Violence in the Workplace

HAWORTH Marketing Resources
Innovations in Practice & Professional Services
William J. Winston, Senior Editor

New, Recent, and Forthcoming Titles:

Market Analysis: Assessing Your Business Opportunities by Robert E. Stevens, Philip K. Sherwood, and J. Paul Dunn

Selling Without Confrontation by Jack Greening

Persuasive Advertising for Entrepreneurs and Small Business Owners: How to Create More Effective Sales Messages by Jay P. Granat

Marketing Mental Health Services to Managed Care by Norman Winegar and John L. Bistline

New Product Screening: A Step-Wise Approach by William C. Lesch and David Rupert

Church and Ministry Strategic Planning: From Concept to Success by R. Henry Migliore, Robert E. Stevens, and David L. Loudon

Business in Mexico: Managerial Behavior, Protocol, and Etiquette by Candace Bancroft McKinniss and Arthur A. Natella

Managed Service Restructuring in Health Care—A Strategic Approach in a Competitive Environment by Robert L. Goldman and Sanjib K. Mukherjee

A Marketing Approach to Physician Recruitment by James Hacker, Don C. Dodson, and M. Thane Forthman

Marketing for CPAs, Accountants, and Tax Professionals edited by William J. Winston

Strategic Planning for Not-for-Profit Organizations by R. Henry Migliore, Robert E. Stevens, and David L. Loudon

Marketing Planning in a Total Quality Environment by Robert E. Linneman and John L. Stanton, Jr.

Managing Sales Professionals: The Reality of Profitability by Joseph P. Vaccaro

Squeezing a New Service into a Crowded Market by Dennis J. Cahill

Publicity for Mental Health Clinicians: Using TV, Radio, and Print Media to Enhance Your Public Image by Douglas H. Ruben

Managing a Public Relations Firm for Growth and Profit by A. C. Croft

Utilizing the Strategic Marketing Organization: The Modernization of the Marketing Mindset by Joseph P. Stanco

Internal Marketing: Your Company's Next Stage of Growth by Dennis J. Cahill

The Clinician's Guide to Managed Behavioral Care by Norman Winegar

Marketing Health Care into the Twenty-First Century: The Changing Dynamic by Alan K. Vitberg

Fundamentals of Strategic Planning for Health-Care Organizations edited by Stan Williamson, Robert Stevens, David Loudon, and R. Henry Migliore

Risky Business
Managing Employee Violence in the Workplace

Lynne Falkin McClure, PhD

The Haworth Press
New York • London

The Haworth Press, Inc., 10 Alice Street, Binghamton, NY 13904-1580

Library of Congress Cataloging-in-Publication Data

McClure, Lynne Falkin.
    Risky business : managing employee violence in the workplace / Lynne Falkin McClure.
      p.   cm.
    Includes bibliographical references and index.
    ISBN 0-7890-0100-4 (alk. paper).
    1. Violence in the workplace. I. Title.
HF5549.5.E43M39   1996
658.4'73–dc20   96-4070
                                                                  CIP

This book is dedicated, with love, to
my husband, Pat, who suggested that I draw this map;
my spirit-sister, Diana,
who rekindled and nurtured this journey;
and
my son, Shawn, who is making his own path.

–LFM

ABOUT THE AUTHOR

Lynne Falkin McClure, PhD, is a management consultant, workshop designer/facilitator and public speaker in Tempe, Arizona. President of McClure Associates Management Consultants, Inc., since 1980, she specializes in work relationships. Dr. McClure began helping client organizations prevent potential violence long before it became the issue it is today. She conducts in-house workshops for corporations and agencies, and speaks at conferences. Through The McClure Institute™ in Tempe, she offers intensive courses for executives, directors, and managers, and for EAP specialists and mental health professionals, on how to identify and prevent potential violence in their own organizations. You may reach her at:

P.O. Box 40637
Mesa, AZ 85274-0637
Phone: (602) 829-6801
Fax: (602) 968-5897
e-mail: lfmcclure@aol.com

CONTENTS

Foreword

In a world that is increasingly dangerous due to the proliferation of regional wars and political terrorism, it is all the more unfortunate that a new enemy–the violent person at work–further fuels our sense of insecurity.

What makes this issue all the more compelling is that the violence does not happen to "someone else in a foreign country"–*this* crime is perpetrated by the former employee, vendor, or customer. It often is ruthless in scope and lethal in its execution. And–shame on *us*– often the violence could have been predicted if our listening and observation skills were just a bit more astute.

In this important work, Dr. Lynne McClure offers a realistic assessment of the causes and management of workplace violence. Her contributions to the field are noteworthy because, although her academic and professional credentials are well established, she writes at a practical level designed to motivate every reader, from the office worker worried about a stalker to a CEO concerned about a hostage and extortion threat.

When I first wrote *Crisis in Organizations* (ITP, 1993), I interviewed nearly forty victims of workplace violence. Their stories horrified and depressed me: here were office managers, executives, secretaries, production workers, pilots–people from every walk of life–who had been shot, stabbed, threatened, raped, punched, or held hostage at work.

One woman, a restaurant manager in her fifties, had been a victim of workplace violence three times in her twenty-year career–merely because of the conditions of the neighborhoods where her only gainful employment could be found. Sometimes the root causes are geographical, sometimes they stem from a vendetta or from mental illness, and sometimes they are shaped by economics. Regardless of the source, they always are destructive.

Is this problem overexaggerated, as some have suggested?

Statistically, it's easy to dismiss workplace violence by analyzing the incident-per-worker ratio, which is modest. But, as the author points out, statistics offer no comfort for victims. More women on the job die from workplace violence than from any other cause, including industrial accidents. For senior executives who are eager to reduce their budgets with layoffs, the decision process now often includes adding security, beefing up psychological counseling, and contracting with outplacement services–often out of fear that a single disgruntled employee could try to harm those who made such decisions.

In early 1995, I was delivering a seminar on workplace violence at a large auto factory in Flat Rock, Michigan. The management team was worried about rumors of violence. Several minor incidents already had occurred. As we discussed the warning signs of a potentially violent person, and as we engaged in an intense simulation of a violent incident, reality struck just two miles away.

There, at the very moment we were trying to convince senior management that workplace violence *was* their problem, three of their colleagues were shot and killed by a disgruntled worker at a sister plant. When the news reached us at the noontime break, people wept for coworkers they had never met. All of a sudden, *statistics* were important; *signals* were important, *learning* was important.

Lynne Falkin McClure adds to our collective learning curve with this important book. Her call to action is rich in substance and grounded in reality.

We must listen.

Larry Barton, PhD
Author, *Crisis in Organizations: Managing
and Communicating in the Heat of Chaos*
and *Ethics: The Enemy in the Workplace*

Preface

This is a tough time for managers to take care of business.

Everyone at work feels stressed. Layoffs are painful, even when they're packaged as "downsizing." Rapid changes make it hard to keep up with technology. Younger workers want *fun* on the job while their seniors worry about *security*. Volatile economic and political conditions worldwide mean more rapid changes in business. Diverse cultures–with conflicting values and life-styles–work more closely together than ever. Baby-boomers experience menopause and midlife *en masse*, affecting their moods and performance at work. The demand for individual choices increases, yet fewer real options exist. Reorganization means more work but fewer promotions. The Americans with Disabilities Act protects the disability of mental illness. Young employees comprise the first generation systematically and electronically entertained by, and desensitized to, violence. Gang members get jobs and pressure their coworkers to steal for them. Many employees go home and face issues of drugs, crime, gangs, abuse. Workers in the United States feel a sense of powerlessness that is new to them.

And individuals act out their rage at work.

Early in 1993, the *thirtieth* U.S. Post Office employee in ten years was murdered by a former coworker. In 1992, homicide was the leading cause of death in the workplace in New York City, the second leading cause in the nation, and the number one cause for women. Employees have committed suicide and left notes blaming their managers. *Surviving relatives have sued these managers as well as the employers.*

Estranged husbands show up with handguns at their former wives' workplaces. Fired employees "return" with guns and kill their former managers and coworkers. "Normal" people go berserk and see the workplace as an outlet, more reachable than the uncontrollable forces outside. Problems at work become the "last straw" of feeling humiliated. The workplace becomes a place to get even.

As a manager, you don't know what form it will take. When it will happen. What will trigger it. Who it will be. How to stop it. If *you'll* be the victim, the scapegoat, the target, or the one who happens to be in the line of fire. If one of your employees will get hurt. Or *do* the hurting.

Dangerous behaviors at work have replaced performance problems as the key issue facing management today. This is a time for a strange mix of compassion and fear. You need to learn how to keep the workplace free of dangerous behaviors; how to protect your employers, your employees, and yourself; how to create, and keep, a positive image of your organization; and how to market your products and services after a crisis occurs where you work.

This book is a guide to recognizing when an employee *is*, or is *becoming*, dangerous. It tells you what your risks are as a manager or supervisor; what you *must* do, and what you *must not* do; and what steps to take to protect everyone involved. It explains *how to recognize the symptoms early enough to prevent a crisis or tragedy.*

Being unaware in the workplace today is *risky business.* Lowering the risk is part of every manager's role in the normal course of "taking care of business."

Acknowledgments

For all their generous support and guidance, I thank:

Todd McDonald, who researched so many options;

Neil Weiner, who helped me find my path;

Diana Friedman, who breathed creativity into the plans;

Heather O'Brien, Irene Simonetti, Monika Hall, Debbie Maciewjewski, Maria Muto, Pat Horrigan, Gwen O'Connor, Cathy McKee, Bob Ballard, Chuck Sauer, Rick Goeld, Paul Zagnoni, and Pam Roe, who let me check the lay of the land;

Arnie Sabel, who made sure I knew the roads were open;

Larry Barton, who sensed my urgency and pointed to the right highway;

Bill Winston, Bill Palmer, and Bill Cohen, who offered the vehicle;

Patricia Brown, Marylouise Doyle, Sarah Eldred, Sandy Jones Sickels, Dawn Krisko, Peg Marr, Paula Patton, Margaret Tatich, Bill Whitaker, and especially Susan Trzeciak, who helped move the vehicle along; and

All the team members, individual contributors, new-hires, project leaders, operators, trainers, engineers, long-term employees, coordinators, secretaries, administrators, computer jocks, supervisors, lab specialists, social workers, managers, assemblers, technicians, EAP counselors, directors, executives, auditors, designers, and workshop participants in all my client organizations—who continue to point me in the right directions.

Chapter 1

The Manager's Dilemma

As a manager, you face a task for which you've had no training, no practice, no role models, and few resources: identifying and dealing appropriately with the employee who is—or is at high risk of becoming—physically dangerous at work.

Managers always have found it harder to deal with the people side of work than with the technical side. You've taken courses in how to deal with employee conflicts, loners in a team environment, poor performers, difficult personalities, ways to motivate everyone, attendance problems, employees' personal issues affecting their work performance, competition, different goals and agendas. Managers spend many hours learning how to deal with people more effectively.

But now it's even harder. You face not only the familiar problems employees present, but also the unfamiliar, seemingly unpredictable risk of employees who are, or may become, *dangerous* at work. Few managers have the information or skills to deal confidently—or appropriately—with high-risk employees.

It is a risk you cannot afford to ignore.

Murder is the number one cause of death for women at work, and the number two cause for men at work. According to the National Institute for Occupational Safety and Health, an average of twenty-one Americans are murdered each week at work (Rymer, 1996).

From July 1992 to July 1993, more than two million workers in the United States were attacked in the workplace, and six million more were threatened with physical violence, according to a 1993 study by Northwestern National Life Insurance Co. Of the workers surveyed in the study, 15 percent said they had been attacked on the job at some point in the overall time they had been working–and for 18 percent of them, with a lethal weapon.

Workplace violence is the fastest-growing type of homicide in the nation. According to the Justice Department, almost one million violent crimes occur in the workplace every year (Kennish, 1995). Further, in an American Management Association survey of 311 companies, almost one-quarter said that since 1990, one or more workers had been attacked or killed at work (Rigdon, 1994). The same survey showed that only 24 percent of these firms had any formal training in dealing with workplace violence and less than half had procedures to cope with violence on the job.

In 1992, homicide accounted for 17 percent of all occupational deaths in the United States, overall ranking second to vehicle accidents but ranking as the number one cause of death for women in the workplace (Purdy, 1994). Although more than three-quarters of the homicides were related to robberies, at least one of these robberies involved the murder of an employee by a coworker.

In addition, domestic problems are the most frequently occurring motive for homicide at work (LaBar, 1994). Although many of the women victims were murdered by men with whom they'd had personal relationships and who were not necessarily coworkers, *all* employees were at risk the moment the murderer was able to enter the workplace unsuspected and unchallenged. Employers and employees have come to expect managers to identify and prevent such threats.

Making it tougher for managers, survivors of employees murdered at work have "won sizable sums in civil suits against employers or others with responsibilities in workplaces" (Purdy, 1994). "Others" may include contractors, security firms, and armored car companies providing services to those employers– and individual managers within the firm as well. In fact, the same article says that survivors have accused employers specifically of "negligent hiring practices or other issues which may have been related to homicides at work." Individual managers may be held responsible for specific acts of negligence, especially if they were involved in the hiring.

There also is some concern that "employers will be made to bear an unreasonable share of the responsibility for protecting their workers or forced to use expensive [measures]" (Purdy, 1994). In 1993, for example, Florida became the first state to legislate security measures for convenience stores–including the requirement that no employee work alone. Individual store owners are responsible for the cost of these measures. "Unreasonable" or not, employers–and individual managers–already are beginning to bear responsibility for something they know very little about.

High-risk employees can create problems for managers and employers even without committing murder. "Negligent hiring" claims have been filed against employers in situations where the *presence* of a "dangerous" employee led to physical and/or mental suffering on the part of other employees ("Workplace Violence," 1992). Just as mental and some forms of physical suffering are hard to measure, the manager may have trouble knowing when a dangerous employee may create this suffering simply by being present. Worse, individual managers who hired such an employee also could be identified as contributing to the suffering. *Customers* could make the same claims about workers they encounter in your store, plant, or office. And even if they don't, what happens to your company's image if a violent incident, or even a lawsuit, brings negative publicity to your organization?

Ironically, the most likely targets of workplace violence have been workers and supervisors in human resources–some of the very people whose responsibilities include resolving employee issues (Kurland, 1993). If even these specialists have trouble identifying a high-risk employee, it is clear that this is a challenge to *all* managers.

As a manager, you are caught in a dilemma: you and your employer must provide a safe work environment for employees, *even though you have not known how to identify "high-risk" individuals nor predict dangerous behaviors*. Just as "ignorance of the law is no excuse," ignorance of the risk will not protect anyone from dangerous behavior at work. Nor will it protect you from the responsibility of managing the risk.

You, as a manager, must look at your employees' behaviors in new ways: how high-risk are their behaviors at work? How can you tell, based on their daily actions, when—and which—employees are more likely to become violent at work? And what can you do to prevent the violence *before* it happens?

The following chapters will show you.

REFERENCES

Kennish, J. W., "Violence in the Workplace," *Professional Safety*, June 1995, pp. 34-36.

Kurland, O. M., "Workplace Violence," *Risk Management*, June 1993, pp. 76-77.

LaBar, G., "Employee Safety Under Fire," *Occupational Hazards*, November 1994, pp. 23-26.

Purdy, M., "Workplace Homicides Provoking Negligence Lawsuits and Security," *The New York Times*, February 14, 1994, sec. A:1, B:2.

Rigdon, J. E., "Companies See More Workplace Violence," *The Wall Street Journal*, April 12, 1994, sec. B:1,9.

Rymer, R., "Murder in the workplace," *Self*, January 1996, pp. 108-111, 130, 131.

"Workplace Violence," *HR Magazine*, December 1992, pp. 81-82.

Chapter 2

The High-Risk Profile:
How to Identify
Potentially Violent Employees

GENERAL CHARACTERISTICS
OF HIGH-RISK EMPLOYEES

Statistics and jargon do not capture the feeling, the nature, the slippery, and indistinct boundaries of high-risk behavior–behavior that means a person is more likely than others to become harmful to himself or herself and/or others.

High-risk profiles can come in many forms. And because the high-risk employee's *general* behavior may seem like anyone else's, it's easy to miss the clues.

So far, little information is available about behaviors, traits, or circumstances that could predict who might become dangerous at work. One article states, "Roughly 80% of homicides are committed by white males who typically are poor performers or loners, have a fascination with guns, have threatened to act violently and have been working at a company for about five years" (Berry, 1994).

Another article lists ten behaviors as "warning signs" (Hofman, 1993):

- Overreaction to changes in corporate policy;
- Threats to coworkers or supervisors;
- Closing out or withdrawing large amounts of money from corporate credit unions;

- Repeated violations of corporate policy;
- Expression of an "everyone is against me" attitude;
- Referring to previous acts of violence, such as spouse or child abuse;
- Expression of a "plan to solve everything;"
- Increased mood swings;
- Increased signs of alcohol or drug abuse; and
- Referring to weapon use, bragging about owning weapons, and "declarations of proficiency" in using weapons.

Hofman quotes a speaker's description of characteristics of high-risk individuals:

- Middle-aged white men;
- Bitter and dissatisfied;
- Suffering from depression or potentially suicidal;
- Frustrated with having only low-level tasks to do;
- Frustrated professionals;
- Refuse to take responsibility for their own problems;
- Have pent-up rage;
- Have little or no support systems;
- Tend to like firearms.

Still another article describes workers who are most likely to commit violence (Kurland, 1993):

- Loner types;
- Suffering from low self-esteem; and
- Working in an authoritarian type of management environment.

A fourth article puts the high-risk employee in a younger age group in its description of the characteristics of violent workers (Gillespie, 1994):

- Male;
- Fifteen to twenty-four years old;
- A history of violence;
- Paranoid-schizophrenic personality disorders, chronic anger, etc. (sic);
- Below-average intelligence;
- Problems dealing with anger and fear;
- An interest in weapons;
- Alcohol or drug abuse;
- A background of family violence;
- A peer group that endorses violence;
- Job instability;
- Influence from the popular culture portrayed on television and in the media.

Like these articles, two recent books (Mantell, 1994; Baron, 1993) describe traits in terms that are vague and general. The books also describe the traits in the jargon of psychological diagnosis—which no manager is qualified to do.

The warning signs in these articles and books include normal actions (such as withdrawing money from a credit union account), manic actions (threats; mood swings; bragging; having a "plan to solve everything"), depressed actions (increased substance abuse; loner types) and perhaps even psychotic, or out-of-touch with reality, actions (paranoid-schizophrenic personality disorder, "everyone is against me"; loner types; having a "plan to solve everything").

But by themselves, only a few of these behaviors (threats, repeated violations of corporate policy, or overreactions to policy changes) may raise a manager's suspicions. In addition, the manager may not have the training required to identify some of these traits (depression, paranoid-schizophrenic personality disorder, feelings that "everyone is against me," pent-up rage, chronic anger) nor the opportunity to know enough about other behaviors (an employee removing money for a credit-union account). And, worse, by the time an employee makes "threats to coworkers or supervisors" or starts "referring to weapon use," he or she *already is dangerous and no longer simply at high-risk of becoming so.* Managers must identify employees at the high-risk stage, *before* they become dangerous.

PATTERNS OF HIGH-RISK BEHAVIOR

To prevent a crisis or tragedy at work, managers need specific, observable, and measurable indicators of the high-risk employee. The following list briefly describes eight patterns of warning signs you can look for every day: specific behaviors that indicate a high-risk employee *could, under stress,* become dangerous. The level of stress that would make a high-risk employee *become* dangerous varies with each employee. But these patterns of high-risk behaviors give you a consistent, objective way to identify the warning signals:

- The *more* of these behavior patterns an employee demonstrates;
- The *more often* the employee demonstrates them; and
- The *more intensely* the employee carries out these patterns, the higher the risk that the employee *could* become dangerous.

These patterns of behavior will help you identify *which* employees to watch more closely, and *when.*

The patterns of high-risk behaviors are outlined below. The following chapters describe each pattern in detail.

The Actors: Employees Who Act Primarily on the Basis of Their Emotions

1. The employee acts on *impulse,* instead of planning what to do, meeting others' expectations, or relating to others' work activities and agendas.

2. The employee *acts out* feelings, especially anger, instead of talking about feelings or dealing with the source of the anger.
3. The employee has *outbursts* of rage, instead of discussing and solving problems as they come up.
4. The employee *overreacts* to situations and people, instead of having a broad perspective or a problem-solving approach.
5. The employee has *exaggerated mood-swings*, instead of a more even-tempered or predictable range.

The Fragmentors: Employees Who See No Continuity Between Actions and Results

1. The employee sees events as *"fragmented,"* as in a series of isolated slides, instead of seeing how past events led to what happens in the present and the future, or how the present and future came out of what happened in the past.
2. The employee sees *time as "frozen,"* and focuses only on *now*, instead of experiencing time as moving and bringing changes with it.
3. The employee *repeats* the same mistakes, instead of learning from them.
4. The employee sees *no* relationship between actions and consequences, instead of realizing that actions have effects and outcomes, and that the effects and outcomes came from things he or she did.

The Me-Firsts: Employees Who Focus Almost Exclusively on Their Own Needs

1. The employee has an *infant-like* awareness only of self, instead of recognizing others' needs or trying to fulfill them.
2. The employee *blames* others, instead of taking responsibility for his or her part of a problem.

3. The employee conveys a *grandiose, omnipotent* self-image, instead of recognizing his or her limitations, shortcomings, or problems.
4. The employee seeks *immediate* gratification, instead of taking steps to achieve it.

The Wooden Sticks: Employees Who Approach Life Inflexibly

1. The employee demands *perfection*, instead of working out reasonable compromises.
2. The employee *rigidly* sticks to specific behaviors, instead of adapting to the situation or the people involved.
3. The employee acts in an *"either-or"* way, instead of looking for options or alternatives between the two extremes.
4. The employee tries to *control* people and events, instead of letting others make their own choices or letting events unfold on their own.

The Mixed Messengers: Employees Who Behave in Passive-Aggressive Ways

1. The employee acts out and "gets even," *without* acknowledging there is a problem, instead of letting others know when their actions bother him or her.
2. The employee *manipulates* others by hinting or referring indirectly to what he or she wants or feels, instead of talking about it openly.
3. The employee *withdraws, and later gets even*, when things don't go his or her way, instead of directly telling others what he or she feels or wants.
4. The employee *expects* failure and lets it happen, instead of finding ways that would lead to success.

The Escape Artists:
Employees Who Avoid Reality

1. The employee relieves stress through using *addictive* substances and/or activities, instead of taking healthy steps to manage stress.
2. The employee *distances* others, instead of developing appropriate work relationships.
3. The employee finds reality too "*flat*" or boring, instead of accepting the truth, finding real options, and working with them.
4. The employee *exaggerates credit* and *minimizes blame*, instead of taking appropriate credit and responsibility.
5. The employee *lies and deceives* others, instead of telling the truth.

The Shockers: Employees Whose Behaviors
Change Suddenly, Dramatically, and/or for the Worse

1. A depressed employee *suddenly* appears happy, instead of recovering in small steps over a period of time.
2. A generally content employee suddenly appears *withdrawn or depressed*, especially if outward circumstances have not changed, but even if they have.
3. The work performance of a good employee suddenly *declines*, whether or not circumstances could account for the change.
4. The attendance of a reliable employee suddenly becomes *erratic*, whether or not circumstances could account for the change.
5. An employee does something *out of character*, especially if it is dramatic or extreme.
6. An employee does anything *extreme* or inherently dangerous, even if it is something he or she "has always done."

7. An employee who exhibits *high-risk* behaviors is *fired*, even if he or she is fired for reasons *other than* these behaviors.
8. An employee is mistreated by his or her *spouse*, especially if the spouse's behavior fits any of the high-risk descriptions.

The Strangers: Employees Who Behave in Remote or Withdrawn Ways

1. An employee is obsessed with plans.
2. A remote and generally *suspicious* employee focuses on a specific coworker, manager, or customer.
3. A remote and grandiose, *high-control* employee becomes intensely agitated and obsessive.
4. A *moody* employee loses touch with reality.
5. An *isolated* employee cannot concentrate on the present.

The following chapters describe these eight patterns of high-risk behaviors in detail. Everyone does *some* of these behaviors *some* of the time, and most of these behaviors are not, by themselves, dangerous. But in combination, they form patterns that signal *lack of responsibility, lack of self-management*, and *lack of concern for others*–patterns which, under intense stress, easily increase the potential for violence.

CONCLUSION

As a manager, you can't always tell how much stress an employee is under, nor how much is "enough" to make that employee become dangerous. These eight patterns give you guidelines: the more an employee's behaviors fit these patterns, the more often these behaviors occur, and the more intense these behaviors are, the higher the risk that the employee may become violent when under intense stress.

These guidelines tell you which employees to watch more closely and when. Later chapters explain how to be fair about watching your employees, what steps to take to *prevent* a crisis, and what to do *if* a crisis occurs.

REFERENCES

Baron, S. A., *Violence in the Workplace*, Ventura, CA: Pathfinder, 1993.

Berry, K. M., "How to Protect Your Company from Office Violence," *Investor's Business Daily*, March 28, 1994, p. 4.

Gillespie, P., "Violence Takes Aim at Workplace," *The Arizona Republic*, March 13, 1994, sec. H:1-2.

Hofman, M., "Protecting Employees from Workplace Violence," *Business Insurance*, September 13, 1993, pp. 24-25.

Kurland, O. M., "Workplace Violence," *Risk Management*, June 1993, pp. 76-77.

Mantell, M., *Ticking Bombs*, New York: Irwin, 1994.

Chapter 3

The Actors:
Employees Who Act Primarily
on the Basis of Their Emotions

Most employees usually think before they act. No matter how they feel—angry, frustrated, envious, overjoyed, eager, gleeful—they usually moderate strong emotions by thinking first and then choosing appropriate ways to deal with their feelings at work. Sometimes this means they will talk directly to the person with whom they are angry. Sometimes it means they will wait and then deal with their frustration at home, by exercising or participating in another stress-relieving activity. Sometimes it means they will express their joy mildly to one coworker with whom they feel close. The point is that most employees note their feelings and then *think* about how to handle them before doing anything.

But one of the first things you, as a manager, will notice about high-risk employees is that they usually *act, at any moment, according to however they feel at that moment*, without thinking about the effect their behavior will have on others, nor whether it fits the workplace. With these Actors, it doesn't matter whether their emotions are positive or negative—the point is that high-risk employees tend to dominate the work setting with whatever they feel.

High-risk employees show this tendency in five ways.

IMPULSIVE BEHAVIOR

They act on *impulse*, instead of planning what to do, meeting others' expectations, or relating to others' work activities and agendas.

As George walked down the hall to his meeting, he saw Marc leaving the building. He remembered Marc saying he finally got the four-wheel-drive pickup they'd talked about. The meeting would have to wait.

"How about a ride around the lot before you leave?" George asked. He hadn't driven a four-wheel drive for a while. He wanted to get his hands on the wheel.

"You bet," Marc said. "Here, you take the keys." It was fun. Now he'd have to head back to the building and come up with some excuse for being late.

On his way back, he remembered. Today he was in charge of the agenda. They couldn't get started until he showed up.

George's spontaneous impulse would have been great on a day off. But he didn't stop to think of where he was, who was counting on him, nor what his behavior said about his interest in the meeting, in the other participants' issues, or in his career.

Don't be fooled by the fun-loving nature of George's impulse. His *acting* on it just because he felt like it was a foolish and thoughtless move, even though the impulse itself was "harmless." What if George ever had an impulse to do damage, get even, or hurt someone? How likely is he to deal appropriately with that impulse? His specific behavior, in this isolated situation, was, by itself, minor. But what his behavior said about his lack of control, lack of self-management, and lack of concern for others is significant. Acting on impulse, as a form of choosing actions primarily on the basis of feelings, is a high-risk behavior.

FEELINGS ARE ACTED OUT

The employee *acts out* feelings, especially anger, instead of talking about them or dealing with the source of the anger.

Larry couldn't stand the way the boss favored certain co-workers. One coworker got flextime so she could be home with her kids. This was great for the kids, but it meant if components came in after she left, Larry had to unpack them and put them in her bin for her. Sometimes he even had to make the parts that she would have made if she were there. He didn't see anyone doing any special favors for *him*.

Then there was Alex, who got special treatment because of "problems" he had to overcome, whatever that meant. Alex got to do the easy jobs that didn't require heavy lifting. So guess who did all the loading and unloading. Frankly, Larry was sick of it.

So when the machine stalled again, he'd had it. They wanted so much work from him but didn't bother to get him decent equipment. It would only take one piece of metal, right there in that slot, to jam everything up and give him a break for a while.

And at least it would take them some time to figure it out. And maybe to prove that he was the one who did it.

Larry's feelings are understandable. Everyone feels angry and frustrated sometimes, and Larry's situation seems unfair. If he had taken these feelings as signals that he felt overworked, Larry could have told his boss the workload was too big. He could have asked for help. He could have presented the problem for the whole team to solve. He could have gone to Human Resources if nothing else worked.

But instead, Larry *acted out* the anger and frustration he felt. The act of sabotage will hurt his employer, in terms of both repairing the machine and losing time on production. The sabotage could, potentially, hurt another worker who tried to use the machine. And worse, with his tendency to act out whatever he feels whenever he feels it, how long before Larry acts out his anger on another person? Larry shows no control, no self-management, no concern for others.

When someone acts out, instead of talking about, feelings, everyone else is at the mercy of whatever that person's feelings are. Acting out feelings is a high-risk behavior.

OUTBURSTS OF RAGE

The employee has *outbursts* of rage, instead of discussing and solving problems as they come up.

Jen had never liked the new policy, because it meant she had to spend more time doing paperwork and less time dealing with customers. But she learned a long time ago that it didn't help if you spoke up, especially if it was to disagree with something the honchos came up with.

So she just went along with it, resenting every second she had to spend filling out forms. Her coworkers didn't seem to mind, but they were so stupid and so willing to flatter the higher-ups, who cared what they thought. They were lucky she kept her opinions to herself.

Until Linda, the boss's secretary, came prancing up to her with some criticism from the big-wig.

"He needs you to do it this way," Linda said. Or something like that. What Jen noticed more was her better-than-you tone of voice. It was so loud that everyone else could hear her.

Jen had had it. The boss didn't even have the guts to say it himself. He sent his little high-horse prancing over to make Jen look bad to everyone. Jen stood up. She shouted louder than she'd ever heard herself shout. She hit the desk with her fist. She screamed at Linda.

Linda froze with her mouth open. Everyone else looked at Jen. For the moment, Jen felt like she'd won.

Jen undoubtedly will apologize later, and if this were her first outburst, everyone else probably will believe her. If she has done this before, her coworkers probably have learned to accept it. But the pattern is there: Jen keeps her anger to herself, does nothing to fix the problems that make her angry, and will, periodically, vent her rage in short but intense outbursts. She may apologize afterward, but she also will have these outbursts again–and again.

These outbursts frighten everyone at work, lower morale, increase levels of anxiety, and, indirectly, lower the team's performance. And that is the best it gets.

Because they are so intense, unpredictable and out of control, the verbal outbursts signal that *physical* outbursts could happen anytime. While she is venting verbally, Jen feels powerful, strong, in charge, invulnerable. She also feels vindicated, finally getting even for the wrongs she has suffered. This "high" makes her so out of control that there is nothing–only chance–to stop her from switching to physical outbursts.

Day-to-day, Jen may be quiet, soft-spoken, maybe even cooperative. But her periodic outbursts indicate lack of control, lack of self-management, and lack of concern for others. Outbursts are high-risk behaviors.

OVERREACTION

The employee *overreacts* to situations and people, instead of having a broad perspective or a problem-solving approach.

To Brad, the worst thing about this job was dealing with angry clients. And this client had to be the worst he'd seen. In fact, "client" was the wrong word for this guy–Brad ran through a list of the worst words he'd ever heard anyone called, and it still wasn't rotten enough to fit this guy.

First of all, Brad didn't really agree that "client" was

what these slobs should be called in the first place. He'd voiced his opinion on this many times. So many, in fact, that his boss specifically asked him to back off. Well, he had a right to his opinion. Dealing with "the public" or "the constituents" meant he had to put up with creeps like this all the time, while "client" sounded like the people at least had some class. As he had said many times, why should he and everyone else have to put on this big show as if they dealt with decent people? But the top guy said so, and now everyone had to treat these creeps as "clients."

And now this "client" was complaining that he had a right to be on this property and that Brad shouldn't have asked him to leave. Brad knew it was all about power, that the guy knew he was wrong and yet needed to prove himself. Well, Brad would let him prove how stupid he was to argue.

Brad got right in his face, calling him stupid, worthless, a bum, a nut, someone who had to no business being here on this particular property. It was guys like him who were the cause of everything wrong today with society and, in fact, the world. Guys like him didn't even deserve to live. They ought to be. . . .

It was only when his partner joined him that Brad calmed down.

"Let me help," he said. "You take a break."

Brad was disappointed. He'd much rather deal with the guy himself.

Brad's impressions of this client probably match his partner's. Everyone has had similar feelings at times.

But Brad's reaction—what he *did* in response to the *situation*—was out of proportion. Brad failed to distinguish between what he felt and what really was going on. To him, his feelings may have "justified" his behavior.

He obviously treated his client badly. He did the same thing to the agency and all its employees, whom Brad represented to the public. What if someone from the media overheard him? What if his client turned out to have political connections? Or a video camera?

Brad's overreaction is verbal—so far. How much more stressed can he feel before his overreaction becomes physical? He already shows difficulty with control, self-management, and concern for everyone he affects. His overreaction is a high-risk behavior.

MOOD SWINGS ARE EXAGGERATED

The employee has *exaggerated mood swings*, instead of a more even-tempered or predictable range of moods.

Everyone on the team compared notes by now. It had started as a joke, but it turned out to be pretty helpful as a way of tracking Roger's moods and figuring out ways to deal with him.

"Watch out, he's only at '2' today," one team member would say, meaning that Roger's mood was low. Maybe after lunch, maybe the next day, another member would say, "He's up to a '7' now," meaning that Roger's mood had risen quite a bit.

It was important for them to know. If he was in what his teammates called his "suicidal mood," around "0" or "1," it was a bad time to present any ideas or ask for any cooperation. The best thing to do was walk lightly, ask how he was, say you thought it would get better soon, and leave him alone. If you stuck around, you'd hear about his alcoholic father and all his other problems. Sometimes he'd say it just "isn't worth going any further down the path of life anymore." And you wouldn't get any work done.

But if Roger was in his "king mood," around "9" or

"10," you could ask him to do about anything. He'd do it well, come up with terrific ideas about new projects and new ways to do them, and he'd go on a long discourse about the direction the organization should go. Sometimes he'd joke around about different ways "one could, in the hypothetical sense, kill one's father." But mostly he'd get creative about work. He was fun to be with, but you'd better watch out—if you counted on any of the commitments he made, you'd be real disappointed when his mood slid back down. He'd swear he never made any of those plans or promises.

Roger's moods could come from so many possible causes that it's not worth the manager's energy to figure out why he acts this way. More important is the effect Roger has on everyone: he creates an emotional roller-coaster, when everyone else expects a more even keel.

Both extremes of his mood swings present their own problems. No one can count on him, make plans including him, or trust what he promises to do. His changing moods, and their extremes, keep everyone "on edge," unsure of how to deal with him. While all of us make small adjustments as we interact with various coworkers, everyone who deals with Roger has to make adjustments that are bigger and more frequent than most people require. Perhaps without him knowing it, and perhaps without him intending to do it, Roger's moods, in effect, *control* everyone.

Even worse, they make him unpredictable. Might his suicidal "hints" and his murderous "jokes" turn into behaviors? How might his suicide affect his coworkers? Might his murderous feelings turn toward someone at work?

Roger's moods mean he is out of control, cannot manage himself and has no concern or, perhaps, no awareness of, his effect on others. His exaggerated mood swings are high-risk behaviors.

When Actor employees base their actions primarily on how they feel, everyone at work is at the mercy of these employees' feelings. All five ways in which they may exhibit this general behavior are, to the manager, high-risk.

Chapter 4

The Fragmentors:
Employees Who See No Continuity
Between Actions and Results

Employees usually see a strong connection between what they do and what happens because of what they did. They see results as feedback about their actions, gladly take credit for positive results they've produced, and quickly resist blame for negative results they've had nothing to do with. If most employees have any problem in this area, it usually centers around taking responsibility for ineffective *behaviors* without blaming their entire *selves* for poor outcomes. Most employees also have a sense of fairness: most of the time, they don't blame others for negative results that are their own, and they quickly protest if a coworker unjustly blames them. During performance reviews, they expect their reviewers' sense of "what's fair" to match their own.

High-risk employees, however, do not see the connections between what they do at one point in time and what happens at another point in time. Instead, as Fragmentors, they see events as discrete, isolated occurrences, similar to individual photos or slides, standing alone without any connections to the past or any effects on the future. They have trouble planning for the future, because they do not see it until it becomes the present. They usually have trouble with long-term relationships because they don't realize how some of their behaviors affect others. They do not identify with their department or team at work because they do not have any sense of growth nor commitment over time. "Cause" and "effect" have no meaning to them. These employees have trouble taking credit *or* blame, understanding feedback, and owning responsibility for anything they do.

High-risk employees exhibit these tendencies in four ways.

EVENTS ARE PERCEIVED AS FRAGMENTED

The employee sees events as *"fragmented,"* as in a series of isolated slides, instead of as a "videotape," where past events lead to what happens in the present and the future, and the present and future come out of what happened in the past.

> The manager dreaded giving Joe his performance review this afternoon. Based on all the hassle Joe raised in the past, the manager had learned to document carefully—in writing— as well as to speak to Joe about both what he did well and what needed improvement. In that sense, the manager was ready and had the documentation for the whole year.
>
> But Joe was hard to get through to. One time, when a team member reminded him about a part of the project he was supposed to have completed by that day, Joe claimed absolutely no knowledge about it, saying, "You never told me anything about it." Another time, when one of the pieces came back for rework and had his initials on the accompanying slip of paper, Joe denied any responsibility. "I've always made them this way," he insisted. And everyone who ever worked with him swore that Joe had no memory from one day to the next. "We go over the steps, we talk about potential problems, Joe even asks questions," they said, "and the next day, he acts like he never heard of any of it. When you ask him directly, he insists that either the discussion never happened or that different instructions were given."
>
> The manager knew it was tough for another reason—Joe came across as so sincere and straightforward that you were

convinced, while you spoke with him, that either he honestly didn't remember or that it really didn't happen. It was frustrating. When you tried to teach him something new, you had to start over every day.

That's what was so strange about giving him a performance review—the manager knew that Joe would be courteous and nod his head. But he also would challenge anything the manager graded him down on and would deny ever having gotten called on it. Even though the manager would make suggestions today, later on Joe would "remember" a review session that was very different from the one the manager remembered.

Joe very likely believes what he tells people—which is different from a "con artist" who knows very well that he is lying. But because what he believes is false, he upsets his work team in several ways. They cannot count on him to take care of his share of the work, because he may "forget" or "not learn" how to do it next time. He will not own responsibility for mistakes he makes, which means that he cannot, or he refuses to, learn. He negatively affects morale—another outcome for which he very likely would deny responsibility: at first, his team members probably question their own memory or sanity, and over time they simply dismiss most of what he says or does.

Perhaps the most significant thing about Joe's fragmentation is his lack of curiosity or concern—he does not ask why others remember events differently than he does, and he does not marvel at others' ability to learn from their mistakes. It is possible that Joe does not notice either situation.

What if Joe feels angry and picked on and, in his fragmented way, feels compelled to act out his current negative feelings? If he attacked a coworker, would he later own any responsibility for the coworker's injuries or death? More likely, Joe would either blame the coworker or have "no idea" how—*or if*—he ever got involved.

Joe's inability to connect events or to learn from them shows that he lacks control, self-management, and concern for those with whom he works. His fragmentation is a high-risk behavior.

TIME APPEARS TO BE FROZEN

The employee sees time as *"frozen,"* and focuses only on *now*, instead of experiencing time as moving and bringing changes with it.

> Jean heard the same thing everyone else heard at the meeting, all about how everyone was "empowered" to make their own decisions. She chuckled to herself when she thought about it. She'd heard the same thing before, maybe even two or three times, and this was just more of the same.
>
> All you had to do, she knew, was keep doing what you've always done, and pretty soon they'd wise up and decide that everyone was making too many decisions and the only ones who wouldn't get in trouble were the ones who hadn't listened in the first place. So all she had to do was kick back and wait for this to pass.
>
> She was shocked when her coworkers started calling themselves a "team," instead of a department. She was shocked again when they expected her to make plans with the whole team instead of getting instructions from the boss, and again when the boss was no longer the boss, but the "team leader." And once again when she had to call the other teams she worked with her "clients." It was worse when she had to ask her clients what services they wanted from her.
>
> Jean was downright hostile by the time the team members started evaluating each other's work. This was the boss's—

or, should she say, the team leader's–job. When she got her feedback from the other team members, her face turned red but she refused to say anything even at any of the meetings.

This, she knew, was crazy. How long could the company survive with the employees running the show? Everything was upside-down.

Probably the only thing that didn't shock her was the notice that she was on performance probation. With everything gone nuts, who'd expect them to value a good, long-term employee?

Everyone has trouble with change. Some employees have more trouble with it than others. But Jean is even worse off, because she experiences time as "standing still" and therefore does not even realize that change has occurred. Instead, Jean sees everyone acting "crazy," "nuts," or "upside-down" in a setting where only she keeps behaving the way everyone "should."

Even if she had been a good worker in the past, Jean clearly gets in her team's way in the new work environment. She probably lowers both morale and productivity because she acts as if "orders" and hierarchy still rule. She may seem out of touch–because she is. Jean doesn't necessarily "like" the old way better. She simply stays "frozen" in whatever behaviors she originally learned. Because she has no sense of time moving, she can't make adjustments when things change.

Jean's sense of time as frozen–whatever the cause of this sense–presents a potential threat to her employer and coworkers. Her view of time standing still means that "now" is all that matters to Jean. It also means that she is closed to the reality of the *external* world around her and is focused, instead, only on her *internal* impressions and ideas. What if Jean's stress makes her think she must "defend" the organization against the "crazy," "nuts," and "upside-down" people and ideas that are "taking over"? What if she blames everything on her boss, or on several team members? Her exclusive focus on "now" could prevent her from thinking about consequences, and her sense of "defending" the firm against "crazy" employees and ideas could justify anything she wanted to do.

Jean's sense of time as standing still means she has no control over what she does, very little self-management, and no concern for her impact on others. It is a high-risk behavior.

MISTAKES ARE REPEATED

The employee *repeats* the same mistakes, instead of learning from them.

> Al figured this afternoon's meeting with his manager would be about Ellen. Ellen, who ran the video library, told Al yesterday she was tired of his "sexist and personal remarks," whatever that meant. Al figured she had talked to his boss.
>
> What she meant was anyone's guess. All he said was, "How about some exciting videos? The last three training tapes I watched had nothing but male speakers." He thought Ellen's answer was rude and irrelevant.
>
> Even worse, why did she have to go to his boss? The boss already had talked to Al after three other situations involving women, and Al was worried that his boss would think he didn't know how to deal with women.
>
> "Look, Al," his boss had said during the third meeting, "you've got to understand that anything that even hints at sexual interest is off-limits, even if you're just joking. You don't want to get yourself or the company sued over sexual harassment. Just stick to business, be pleasant but not personal or too friendly. And don't make any comments that refer to the fact that they're women."
>
> Al couldn't figure it out. With Alice, his first complainer, all he had said was, "That dress sure shows your figure."

The boss said that was too personal and too clearly about her body.

So when he wanted to give Nancy a compliment, he changed it and said, "You sure look sexy in that outfit." His boss said Nancy had complained and that it was the same problem.

"But I didn't refer to her body," Al answered, confused.

"Look," his boss said, "it's not just the phrasing. Don't talk about their looks or their bodies. That's the safest way to go."

So when he told Rene, "I'd sure like to take you on this business trip with me," he was shocked to learn she had complained to his boss.

"It wasn't about her looks or body," he said, "it was about me. And she knew I didn't mean anything by it. How come no one here can take a joke?"

His boss was pretty disgusted by then. So this was just what he needed—another complaint, this time from Ellen. It wasn't fair. His comment to Ellen wasn't about her looks, her body, or even her. Why were they picking on him?

Whatever the cause, Al clearly repeats the same mistake without realizing it. Each time, the mistake is "new" to him because he experiences each event as unique and discrete, instead of seeing the similarities between them. He has trouble applying his boss's "lessons" to a new situation. Interestingly, this tendency may make Al look ignorant, stupid, willful, defiant, sexist, or sexually obsessed—or all of the above—when at the least his difficulty with changing the pattern comes from his failure to generalize.

By now, Al's presence probably creates fear or anxiety among his female coworkers. His behavior probably hurts his own credibility and lowers morale. He truly presents the risk of lawsuits against his employer, as well as against himself.

Al is a high-risk employee for two reasons: his repetition of the same mistake, regardless of the topic; and his obsessive concentration on the topic of sex.

- His repetition, or inability to generalize and learn, is simply another version of inability to take feedback. Like Jean, above, who is frozen in time, Al is closed to input from the world around him, which means he focuses only on his own internal needs. This self-centeredness puts him at high-risk for repeating the same mistakes, unaware of–and unconcerned about– how he affects the women around him. How can anyone tell where his "interest" in women will stop? Is a woman safe meeting alone with him?
- The topic itself creates more problems. His obsessive concentration on sex makes him appear dangerously out of control. Whether he means it or not, and whether he is aware of it or not, Al conveys the message that he will act out his sexual agenda "no matter what."

Al's repetition of *any* mistakes makes him high-risk. Because his repeated mistakes are in the sexual arena, his behavior is even more high-risk. He appears out of control, lacking in self-awareness about it, and lacking concern for his effect on others–especially women.

LACK OF UNDERSTANDING OF ACTIONS AND CONSEQUENCES

The employee sees *no relationship* between actions and consequences, instead of realizing that actions have effects and outcomes, and that the effects and outcomes came from things he or she did.

Carl knew very well that his boss wanted him to show more interest in customers' needs. The boss sure sent him to enough sales seminars for Carl to figure that out. The problem was, though, the customers weren't as eager as the boss thought they'd be to get a "customer-oriented" sales approach.

All Carl had to do was keep taking orders and hope the boss backed off for a while. His customers knew what the company sold, what they needed, and what to order. Carl didn't see any reason to bother them with questions or take up more of their time.

That's why he was shocked when he learned that Harry, his biggest customer, had started ordering from a competitor. Carl couldn't believe it. He was sure that Harry's secretary had it wrong when she took Carl's phone call and said there was no order for that month, and ended the conversation with, "Why don't you let us call you, instead of you calling us, for now? We have a new supplier."

When Carl called Harry and asked what happened, Harry said, "You shouldn't be so surprised. I've been telling you for months that we're changing our equipment. Your stuff doesn't fit our new machines. Besides, I kept telling you that sometimes the shipments were late getting here, slowing us down. The new guy checks with me every week, to see how our orders are and whether we need to make any changes. He's already helped us cut our cycle time."

Carl felt offended that Harry was so rude to him. How could he blame Carl for cycle-time problems? He'd have to call Harry in a while and see about next month's orders.

Carl takes no responsibility for Harry's dissatisfaction, because he sees no connection between his sales style and Harry's decision to change suppliers. Carl also misses an opportunity to learn about identifying customer needs and the effect of his delivery schedule on production costs. Instead, he takes Harry's comments as an isolated incident, unaware that Harry's needs and Harry's business relationship with him have changed—or that the relationship has changed *because* of him.

Carl may appear naive or even stupid. He may call Harry some time in the future, act as if nothing happened, and literally be surprised again when Harry refuses to place an order. Carl also may repeat the same mistakes with other customers.

Because he doesn't see the relationship between his actions and the consequences, Carl probably sees other people's behavior as random, rather than as reactions to him or as feedback. This "frees" Carl of responsibility for his own behavior. His employer loses both money and a customer, yet Carl considers himself "innocent."

What if, under intense stress, Carl hits a customer or coworker in anger? His behavior already shows that he is unlikely to take responsibility for it or, perhaps, even admit that he did it. More likely, he will say the other person started it, minimize the magnitude of the violence, or passively say that "it happened" as opposed to acknowledging "I did it." Because Carl misses this connection, he is out of control, unable to manage himself, and lacking in concern for others.

When Fragmentor employees see no continuity between their actions and the consequences, they can neither learn nor change. They make it hard for you to hold them accountable for what they do. To managers, all forms of lack of continuity are high-risk behaviors.

Chapter 5

The Me-Firsts:
Employees Who Focus
Almost Exclusively
on Their Own Needs

Most employees have figured out that, as adults, they must negotiate their relationships with others, which means they have to consider other people's needs, as well as their own, when they want to do something. Even in working out conflicts, employees usually know from the start that they will have to compromise. More than just a formality, they know that solutions last longer if all parties "win" in some way. They also know that needs can be motivators, and that by helping—or, sometimes, just by *allowing*—others to get their needs met, they have motivated the others to work out an agreement with them. In daily give-and-take, employees usually see long-term benefits from short-term sacrifices. Even though, like all of us, they'd much rather get their way every time, they realize that giving in a little bit now will pay off in a compromise later.

High-risk employees, however, acknowledge *neither* the other person nor his or her right to exist and have needs. Me-First employees see themselves as the center of the universe, with other people around them simply as "props." Teamwork does not fit their style, because they like getting all the credit when things go well. When there is a mistake or problem, however, high-risk employees would rather blame someone else than take responsibility for fixing it. They also dislike the negotiations required of teams, and prefer to decide or dictate what to do. Even as individual contributors, high-risk employees still have trouble dealing with managers' and clients' needs.

High-risk employees show these tendencies in four ways.

INFANT-LIKE AWARENESS

The employee has an *infant-like* awareness only of himself or herself, instead of recognizing others' needs or trying to fulfill them.

> Brooke knew that taking Friday off meant everyone else would be overloaded for the weekend. Especially since it already was Thursday and no one else could be scheduled to take her place. Besides, she wasn't going to make it official—she'd just call in tomorrow and say she wasn't feeling well, which meant they couldn't have scheduled it anyway. This had to look like it wasn't her choice.
>
> Besides, she'd already been on this job for a month and hadn't called in sick, been late, or asked for extra days off the whole time. They ought to appreciate her dependability. Now she deserved a break.
>
> She remembered that the manager wanted to put her in charge of a special project tomorrow, and she knew the manager was counting on her because of her computer skills. It was a rush job for one of the big customers. Well, they'd just have to wait.
>
> Brooke had the chance of a lifetime tomorrow. James, the brother of her new roommate and the January feature in a popular women's magazine, might come to town to visit his sister. If she hung around, Brooke might get a chance to meet him.

Everyone can understand Brooke's *tentative* "opportunity." But it's more appropriate in high school or middle school than at work, and maybe more acceptable if Brooke is closer to twenty than to forty.

But the real issue is that it's normal for *infants* to be aware only of their own needs and to be oblivious to the needs, and even the existence, of others. This mind-set is *not* all right for adult employees.

Brooke clearly thinks only of herself and what she wants. Even though she realizes the negative effects her plan will have on her coworker, the manager, the big customer, and perhaps later, the company in general, she will carry out her plan anyway. Brooke cunningly will take steps to appear to be "the victim" of an illness when, in fact, she is a predator to those who count on her. She does not see when her own needs have gone too far and she has crossed into an area where others rightfully have expectations of her.

Brooke's behavior says not only that she will watch out for herself, but also that she will take whatever she wants *even at the expense of others at work.* It's pretty clear that if she were under intense stress, Brooke could take it out on a coworker, manager, or customer without much hesitation. Whether she would become violent, and how far she would go, depends more on what *she* needs at the moment than on who is present or what they might expect from her.

Brooke's exclusive focus on her own needs means her behavior is out of control, she lacks self-management, and she has no concern for others. Her focus is a high-risk behavior.

BLAME IS PLACED ON OTHERS

The employee *blames* others, instead of taking responsibility for his or her part of a problem.

Darryl had a lot of explaining to do about this one. He'd all but promised the boss that this deal was as good as closed, and now it had unraveled on him. This was the third time in a row that what looked like an easy sale turned out to be nothing.

"Well, it looked good until one of our competitors came in with a lower price," he told his boss.

"I thought price was not the main issue," the boss said. "You told me they were after quick turnaround time."

"Well, they must have changed their minds," Darryl said. He had forgotten that. Need to pay more attention next time. He hadn't mentioned turnaround time during his presentation.

"Besides," the boss said, frowning, "I thought you said our price was lower, anyway."

Had he said that? "Yes," Darryl said, "I thought it was. I might have misunderstood them. Or else the competition lowered their price." That was a stupid thing to say. No one changes the price in the middle of a bid.

The boss kept frowning. "There seem to be a lot of misunderstandings lately," he said. "What's going on?"

Darryl felt uncomfortable. "Things are tougher out there. It's the whole economy today."

"Yeah, the economy. Nothing anyone can do about that, huh?"

"Nope," Darryl said. He felt relieved. Maybe he got away with this one. He'd better keep more on top of things from now on.

Everyone makes mistakes. But Darryl compounded his mistakes by blaming others instead of taking responsibility for his lack of preparation or his poor follow-through. If his employer is lucky, Darryl will admit to himself that he needs to pay more attention to his accounts, and he'll take appropriate steps to do so. If the employer *isn't* lucky, Darryl will keep blaming others until he loses his accounts. Darryl's behavior already is bad for sales.

His behavior could become worse if Darryl ever gets stressed out. He readily shifts blame and responsibility to others and does not acknowledge his own contribution to problems. Under enough stress—if, for example, his job were on the line—he could become dangerous to someone else whom he blamed: the potential client who won't buy, the boss who won't put up with his poor record, a competitor's salesperson who "steals" customers. Darryl all too readily blames others for situations to which he at least contributes.

Employees who blame others take no responsibility for their behavior, have no self-management, and show no concern for anyone else. Blaming is a high-risk behavior.

EXAGGERATED SELF-IMAGE

The employee conveys a *grandiose, omnipotent* self-image, instead of recognizing his or her limitations, shortcomings, or problems.

> The group knew they'd have to wait a while. Whenever Jim ran this meeting, he made a point of being late. They figured it was his way of flaunting his power. They also knew how much he loved power. He even got a rush from running the meeting—at least, it looked that way.
>
> When he finally showed up, he followed his usual pattern: he spoke for about fifteen minutes straight, emphasizing once again the importance of his department and the good fortune bestowed on everyone else who was lucky enough to work with him and his people. He didn't use those words, of course, but it was what he meant.
>
> Today, Jim had an even more significant fact with which to amaze them.

"I've figured out how to save the company a lot of money," he said. "Let's stop paying for employee tuition. Instead of paying the colleges so much money, we'll have the employees who've already got degrees teach classes in their fields. I can be the first," he said, beaming. Instead of asking what everyone thought of his idea, Jim looked proud as he waited for spontaneous praise.

When people asked, "How can we teach? That's not what we know how to do," and "What about college credits? How can our employees earn degrees that way?" and "That's cheating! Tuition is one of the benefits we offer," Jim simply brushed the air with his hand and smiled. "No problem," he said, "I know people on the Board of the community college. I'll take care of everything."

"That's what I was afraid of," someone said. It wasn't clear who.

Whether he really thinks his plan will help, or he just wants a lot of attention, Jim's motive makes no difference. His *effect* is a problem for his employer, and the more power and influence he has, the more widespread his negative impact will be.

How he communicates—showing up late when he's in charge, bragging about his department, inviting praise about his ideas— may be even worse than *what* he communicates—his "money-saving" plan. Even if his plan didn't put the firm in a vulnerable position, his way of delivering the news puts the emphasis on him instead of on the plan. His casual reference to taking care of everything shows how omnipotent he believes himself to be.

The likelihood that the plan would *hurt* the firm means that Jim values attention more than he values the success of his employer. Despite his reputation, he clearly has a "grandiose" self-image or, at least, wants others to think a lot of him. Day-to-day, Jim's behavior has the capacity to hurt the organization's morale, performance, motivation, teamwork, and if his position is high enough, credibility.

Under the best conditions, Jim—with his infant-like failure to see beyond his own needs—frustrates the other managers. Under intense stress, he might perceive others as failing to appreciate him or depriving him of the "worship" he deserves, and his indifference could turn to hostility. If his infantile anger triggers his adult strength, Jim could be violent—against whomever happens to be there.

Jim's grandiose, omnipotent demeanor means he is out of control, is unable to manage himself, and clearly has no concern for anyone else. His demeanor is a high-risk behavior.

SEEKS IMMEDIATE GRATIFICATION

The employee seeks *immediate gratification*, instead of working toward a goal, and giving it time to develop.

In the two weeks since he started, Dave already had found a few things that should be changed. Fresh out of college, he had great ideas about how companies should run. For starters, the performance review system. It was the same form for the whole organization, and it was too vague. They needed something that focused more on their specific departments.

He knew the system had been in place a long time. He also knew that most employees thought it was okay, but that was only because they didn't know about new developments in the field. But, he figured, why waste time at this level, when big changes like this have to start at the top. So at the end of his second week, he made an appointment with the Vice President of Human Resources.

He was surprised when his manager showed up and said, "The VP wants to know what's up. Anything I can help you with?"

"I didn't want to bother you with it," Dave said, "especially because the decision has to come from higher up. It's an idea I had for a better performance review system. Want to take a look at my suggestions?"

"Maybe sometime," the manager said. "But don't you think you need more than two weeks to start re-engineering the company?"

"One of my papers was on performance reviews," Dave answered, taking the question literally. "I know how to evaluate and improve them."

"I just thought it might help you to take more time, see how things run, get in on the grapevine, hear what your people tell you. You know, get to know the culture here, so to speak." The manager tried to be supportive.

"Well, how about this," Dave said. "After I see the VP, I'll let you know what the next step is. I think these changes need to be put in place quickly, so employees can be more motivated and the firm can stay ahead of the competition."

Dave may mean well, but he comes across as either extremely naive or too ambitious politically. Ironically, any ambition he has will be hurt by his lack of awareness of how organizational politics work. Dave broke the chain of command and acted as if he were the "expert" instead of the newcomer both to the industry and the company.

Eager to achieve and succeed immediately, Dave probably alienated both his manager and the vice president in the process. On the surface, he has the potential to be a young, bright star in the company. *If* he learns how to pay his political dues, *if* he can get short-term gratification often enough, and *if* things go well for the firm, Dave probably can fulfill this potential.

But if Dave is stressed past his limits—because these conditions are not met, or for some other reason—his need for immediate gratification may push him to do *something* that gives him closure. He does not wait well for things to happen on their own.

A violent act may contain both the satisfaction of closure and the gratification of immediacy. Dave's tendency to seek immediate gratification means he easily loses control, does not manage himself, and is unaware of how he affects others.

His tendency to seek immediate gratification is a high-risk behavior.

When Me-First employees focus almost exclusively on their own needs, *at their best* they are indifferent to everyone else. Under intense stress, they see others as either sources of frustration or blocks to their desires. They show lack of control over their behavior, inability to manage themselves, and no concern for the people around them.

To managers, all four ways employees focus almost exclusively on themselves are high-risk behaviors.

Chapter 6

The Wooden Sticks:
Employees Who Approach Life Inflexibly

Everyone has some trouble dealing with change and with differences, and with the adjustments both require.

Most employees, however, know that change keeps coming, and they learn how to adapt as it comes. They take classes to learn about new computer systems. They work together, with facilitators, to figure out how to work as a new team. They learn the specifics about a new job responsibility. Many learn to see change as exciting and as a source of opportunities. But even those who dread the change vent to their friends, learn more about the change, and eventually adapt.

Most employees deal the same way with differences. At first, they may not accept ways other people act, dress, or work that are different from their own. But over time they learn more about the individuals and, eventually, understand and accept the differences, whether or not they want that style for themselves. In handling change and differences, most employees learn and adjust.

But high-risk employees have more trouble than others in dealing with both change and differences. To Wooden Sticks, change means personal *criticism* and *rejection* of "the way we've always done things." And they experience differences as *challenges* or *threats* to their own ways of acting, dressing, or working. Instead of learning and adapting, high-risk employees approach life inflexibly. They see change and differences as challenges to their individual identity and, therefore, as things they must resist, prevent, or fight. High-risk employees act out their inflexibility in four ways.

PERFECTIONISTS

The employee demands *perfection*, instead of working out reasonable compromises.

> Ronnie knew what the law said, but she didn't see why she had to put up with it when so many people were applying for jobs. She finally had the funds to fill a position that had been vacant for nearly a year, and who did Human Resources send her but someone who was deaf.
>
> "The job is keeping track of inventory. You know, a lot of communication with the people in the warehouse and front desk," she complained to her coworker Mel. "How is a deaf person going to do that?"
>
> "I understand that Vera reads lips and speaks fluently. There shouldn't be any problem," Mel said.
>
> "Well, what if she gets phone calls?" Ronnie asked.
>
> "I've seen a screen that shows messages in print," Mel answered. "They also make a keyboard that Vera could use to send messages over the phone."
>
> Ronnie shook her head. "That's a lot of trouble and expense to go to, isn't it? I mean, if she can't hear, then why do we have to put her in this kind of job? Isn't there something she can do that doesn't require talking or listening?"
>
> "Or breathing?" Mel laughed. "You think she spends her life not dealing with anyone? Where've you been? Joe in the warehouse uses a support belt because of back problems, Mary uses the handicapped parking because of her foot, Steve uses the keyboard a special way because he's missing two fingers, and Martin has dyslexia so he's taking that reading class. So what if Vera needs some equipment?"

Ronnie frowned. "I just don't get it. Lots of people out there don't have limitations or special needs. Why do we hire people with imperfections?"

Clearly unaware of her own—and, in fact, of *everyone's*—"limitations" and "imperfections," Ronnie has an unrealistic standard for her employees. Her ideas may come from ignorance, prejudice, fear, guilt, some personal sense of shame, or some combination of these. Whatever the source, Ronnie prefers the delusion of "perfect" people—presumably including herself—over the reality that we all have limitations even though some are less visible than others. Ronnie's demand for perfection denies the fact that all of us try for reasonable compromises to make up for something we don't do easily.

Even worse, Ronnie's perfectionism leads to a ranking system where, to her, disabled persons are "less than"—that is, less *human* than—those who are "perfect." The "faulty" person becomes an *object* to Ronnie. Under intense stress, might she use such an "object" as an outlet, much like a punching bag or a wall? Her assumption that she is perfect may, to her, justify this kind of action. And because we all have limitations, no one would be safe.

Ronnie's perfectionism means she is out of touch with—and thinks she is above—the truth about people. Her perfectionism is a high-risk behavior.

RIGID BEHAVIORS

The employee *rigidly* sticks to specific behaviors, instead of adapting to the situation or the people involved.

Russ had gotten a lot of coaching about this problem, but his team leader insisted on talking about it some more on the way to the meeting.

"The three people we're meeting with know a little about the phone system you want them to set up," the team leader said. "So you don't have to start from scratch. But at the same time, don't assume they know very much about what you want, either. Just explain how you want to be able to use the phones, you know, what you want the phones to do, and let them come up with their own design."

"I know, I know," Russ said. "'Don't talk down to them,' 'don't get impatient if you have to say it over,' and 'don't tell them how to do their work.' I swear, I could teach that communication course myself by now."

The team leader laughed. "Yes, but can you use all that when you're face-to-face with them? That's what we're after."

At the meeting, Russ looked at the drawings they handed him.

"Now, these are just preliminary drawings," they said, "just to give us a starting point. Tell us the specifics you need and we'll mark the drawings accordingly."

"I can't use this kind of setup," Russ said, frowning. "It's got too many lines for one person to handle. And I can't tell from this whether someone could listen in on a call."

"Sure. But, remember, these are just the preliminaries. So it sounds like one thing you need is private lines. And do you want to limit the number of lines, or do you want to have more than one station where they can be answered?" One of the team members wrote notes on the drawings.

Russ sighed, still frowning. "Didn't we talk about this already?" he asked.

"You and I talked," the team leader said. "But this has not been discussed in the group."

"Hmmm," Russ said. "Well, let's continue. Where on the drawing does it show the lines with conference capability?"

On the way back, he told the team leader, "It's important to check everything. When you have to spell things out like that, you just can't count on them doing a good job."

Russ acts as if the group already knows his needs, the drawings should be complete, and the group has done an inadequate job–despite the team leader's reminders, and the group's assumption, that this is a data-gathering meeting in the early stages of the project. Instead of adjusting to the actual situation and the people involved, Russ sticks to his assumptions and acts accordingly.

Like so many other high-risk behaviors, the way Russ rigidly keeps acting as if his assumptions were accurate may not, by itself, seem significant. But it says a lot about the way Russ deals with others: he is closed to feedback and has no interest in, nor awareness of, other people's needs nor agendas. Instead, he operates strictly from his own assumptions, rigidly focusing on his own internal needs and goals *without considering the real circumstances or the other people around him.* As if driving a car with his eyes closed, Russ acts upon the world without checking to see how he is doing and without adjusting to "stops" or "curves" he encounters.

If he were under extreme pressure, Russ's rigid, unchanging behavior literally could "run over" others. Unable to tell or care when he hurts someone and unable to sense when he's gone too far, Russ could become violent if he assumed his needs were threatened.

His tendency to hold on rigidly to specific behaviors instead of making adjustments is a high-risk behavior.

"EITHER-OR" BEHAVIOR

The employee acts in an *"either-or"* way, instead of looking for options or alternatives between the two extremes.

Jason knew exactly how to put together the presentation. First, focus on the product's features and, second, show how many ways these features could benefit the customer. In his mind, he outlined the features and benefits as he drove to work. He couldn't wait to tell his boss.

But his boss didn't want to hear about it. "This is a team project," the boss said. "Give your ideas to your teammates. Everyone should be in on all the decisions."

"Sure, the team," Jason answered. "But I thought if you got a preview first. . . ."

"No, no previews. I'll see it when the team has decided."

Jason told the rest of the team about his ideas. "Features first, to catch the customer's interest, and then the benefits. Two simple steps."

"What about the customer's needs? That should come before the features," one of the team members said.

"Yeah, first show the customers we know what they're after," said another teammate. "Then show the product features."

"That'll get their attention faster," said another member.

Jason shook his head. "No, that's too predictable. It'll catch them off-guard to get hit with the features first."

"How about this," said one of the teammates. "Let's do mock-ups both ways, and see how they strike us. It'll be easier to decide if we see how it looks both ways, instead of just describing each way."

"Good idea," said a few others.

"No," said Jason, standing up. "We don't need to bother with all that. We've seen enough presentations to envision each way. Let's just decide."

"Well, I, for one, could tell better by seeing mock-ups," one member said. "That way, I can put myself in the customer's position and see how it strikes me overall." Others agreed.

"No, we don't need to."

"Jason, what's the big deal?"

"Look," Jason said, still standing, "it's got to be features first so it will be unusual, catchy. It's pretty obvious what the right decision is."

Jason shows "either-or" behavior in several ways. He sees only one way to design the presentation—and is so convinced that he even tries to get his boss's support before presenting his ideas to his team. Jason won't consider anyone else's point of view. By refusing to go along with the mock-ups, he shows an urgency about getting his own way—so much so that it becomes unclear whether his insistence is more about the presentation or about who wins.

No wonder Jason feels so urgent. His "either-or" actions lead to "win-lose" situations, with glory going to the winner, and shame, humiliation, and loss of status going to the loser. In a team decision, Jason appears to have a lot more at stake, emotionally, than simply how the presentation should look.

If a simple decision for a routine assignment creates so much pressure for Jason, how might he act in more demanding situations? Under enough stress, fearing what he sees as loss and its accompanying humiliations and threats to his identity, Jason may stop at nothing to protect his pride.

Acting in "either-or" ways is a high-risk behavior.

CONTROLLING PERSONALITY

The employee tries to *control* people and events, instead of letting others make their own choices or letting events unfold on their own.

It was time for Bob to make his "rounds," as he called them, again. With all the stuff happening, and all the rumors starting, he had to make sure his friends knew the latest. He owed it to them.

First, he told Carol. She was such a sweet person that others might take advantage of her if she didn't know what was going on.

"Carol, have you heard about the move?" he asked.

"What move?"

"Your department. You'll all be moving to the other location in a few months. I wanted you to know so you could get ready."

"What?" Carol was stunned. "There's no room for us there. Why would we move, anyway? It doesn't make sense."

"I don't know the whole story, but what I hear is that this department is going to be a lot smaller. You know, after the reorganization. And everyone who's still in it will move over to a smaller space."

"Smaller?" Carol's face turned red. Bob felt so bad for her. She looked like she didn't know what to do. "Do you mean there'll be layoffs? Do you know who'll be laid off?"

"Well, nothing for sure," Bob said. "But here's what I think you should do. You know that new public relations guy—Pete, I think's his name—you might go talk to him, see if he's able to use you. You never know."

Carol nodded her head, still red-faced and looking shocked. "Bob, you are such a big help. I won't tell anyone. I can't believe it, after all the time I've. . . . I'll have to think about this first. I can't just barge into Pete's office and apply for a job. I don't even have a resume. I've got to let all this sink in. How did you find out?"

Bob smiled. "Look, I wouldn't wait too long."

He spread the word, telling several friends how they would be affected by the upcoming changes and what he thought they should do. Bob felt proud by the end of the day. He probably saved a few jobs for his friends. And probably saved them a lot of worry, too.

Within a few days, Bob's boss called him in.

"I understand you've been up to the rumors again," the boss said. "Just like the two times before." He looked at papers on his desk. "You've been told before–the false rumors hurt morale and performance in several departments, and we can't tolerate that. We said all this to you twice already. I even got a call from Pete yesterday, asking what was going on. I don't want any explanations. Just go to Human Resources. They'll go over your record and explain the paperwork. And they'll tell you about the outplacement policy."

Bob was furious. He knew the "rumors" were facts and that he was being set up because one of the reasons for the "reorganization" was to eliminate Carol's job. The same was true about some of his other friends.

Well, he wasn't one to let things just happen. He'd have to see what he could do for himself now.

Bob is very explicit about *what* Carol should do, but not *why*. By giving her only part of what he's heard, Bob warns her *but also* keeps her dependent on him, willing to do whatever he suggests. Real help would mean telling her the whole situation and letting her make decisions for herself.

Even if the rumors Bob hears are true, his way of dealing with Carol controls her at least as much as it helps her. If the rumors are not true, his control clearly is out of line. In addition, Bob goes beyond being proactive when he tells Carol specifically where she should apply for a new job.

All of us like a certain amount of control over our lives and our work. But Bob wants control over others, as well, and he is likely to feel stressed when something limits it. Now that the limitations affect his control over his *own* career, how might he react? Typically, violent acts occur within one week after an employee has been fired and threatened to retaliate (Berry, 1994). Violence may make

Bob feel–and look–powerful. Under intense stress, it may appear to him as ultimate control.

For all his attempts to control others, Bob shows very little *self*-control. He also lacks self-management and real concern for others. Controlling others and events is a high-risk behavior.

When Wooden Stick employees act in ways that are rigid instead of flexible, they have trouble adapting to new or challenging situations. Because of their rigidity, they too easily "snap" and go to extremes.

All four ways employees exhibit inflexibility are, to managers, high-risk behaviors.

REFERENCE

Berry, K. M., "How to Protect Your Company from Office Violence," *Investor's Business Daily*, March 28, 1994, p. 4.

Chapter 7

The Mixed-Messengers: Employees Who Behave in Passive-Aggressive Ways

Most of the time, when managers and supervisors are open to it, employees talk directly and straightforwardly about what they need, what problems they've run into, and where they need help. The team approach at work can make straight talk even less political and, therefore, easier. Even when the problems involve the way someone acts towards them, employees usually will let that person know what bothers them. If a communication problem exists for most employees, it's about *how* they say what's on their minds, *not whether* they say it.

But high-risk employees can keep everyone "on edge" and "in the dark," if their words say one thing while their behaviors say something else. The Mixed-Messengers *talk* as if they are part of the team, pleased with activities and outcomes, comfortable with interactions, and oriented toward the same goals as everyone else. But they *act* as if they feel excluded, dislike what is going on, have problems with interactions, and want failure. If anyone asks them what's going on, or points out the discrepancy between what they say and what they do, Mixed Messengers deny all of it. They are aggressive, but in passive ways.

High-risk employees act out their passive-aggressiveness in four ways.

UNACKNOWLEDGED RETRIBUTION

The employee acts out and "gets even," *without* acknowledging there is a problem, instead of letting others know when their actions bother him or her.

Todd showed up late for the third time this week. Linda, the manager, asked him what was going on.

"Hey, I really apologize," Todd said, smiling. "This has been a tough week for my car. All three times, my car's died on me. I know I should call, but I'm out there in traffic trying to fix the stupid thing."

"I understand about not calling," Linda said. "It's just that when you're late, it affects everyone else."

"Oh, I know," Todd said. "Hank's shift is over, but he can't leave till I get here. And it puts more work on the others. I guess I should start out earlier, just in case. But the thing is, when the car dies, I can't tell how long it will take to fix it."

Linda nodded her head. "It's a problem. But tell me, Todd—are you sure it's all about the car?"

"What do you mean?"

"Well, when this week's schedule was posted, you didn't seem too happy about it. And you've been late three times since then, which has never happened before. Is there some connection?" Linda asked.

"No," said Todd, shaking his head. "Not at all. I don't remember being unhappy about the schedule. Did I say something?"

"Not exactly. It was more the look on your face. Does the schedule interfere with your classes?"

"Not really. I mean, I have to rush right out of the Monday and Wednesday class for here. But it's no problem. It's just that, well, when you add my unpredictable car . . ." Todd shrugged his shoulders.

Linda said, "Well, if it's a problem, I can always redo the schedule. It's just that I have to know the same day it's posted."

"Oh, sure. But really, there's no problem with that," Todd said.

Linda sighed. "Okay," she said. "Well, maybe you can do something about the car. I need you to be here when you're scheduled."

"You bet," Todd said, smiling.

Todd's smile and cooperative words make it seem, on the surface, as if his car is the only problem. But he may be *too* smiley, *too* cooperative, and too "innocent." Linda, at least, suspects the real problem is the schedule.

Is Todd "getting even" by inconveniencing everyone? *Does the schedule, or does it not*, interfere with his Monday and Wednesday classes? Did he feel annoyed when the schedule was posted? Does he really not know how he looked, nor remember whether he said anything? Does he really agree with Linda and understand the problems, or is he mocking her?

Maybe—and maybe not. The uncertainty keeps everyone unsure of Todd's motives, how to treat him, how honest he is. He doesn't sound sincere, but he doesn't sound like he's lying, either. It's the inability to know that makes it hard to deal with Todd.

For Todd, keeping others uncertain is a source of power. It keeps them confused and prevents anyone from disciplining him. By going both directions at once, he "keeps 'em guessing" and never has to take responsibility for what he does.

And that's when things are relatively mild. Under intense stress, will Todd get more ingratiating, more "cooperative," *and* more destructive? Might he become violent in a sneaky, unacknowledged way—by, say, poisoning someone's coffee or aspirin? Might even his violence be indirect, aimed at someone *randomly* instead of at the person "causing" his problems? Might it look as if someone else did it?

It's hard to say. And our uncertainty shows us that Todd hides his feelings, rather than managing them. He speaks through his behaviors, rather than controlling himself, and he has little concern for others. Todd's unacknowledged getting even is a high-risk behavior.

MANIPULATION

The employee manipulates others by *hinting or referring indirectly* to what he or she wants or feels, instead of talking about it openly.

Bill felt annoyed when the boss started praising the new employees, right there in the middle of the staff meeting, for taking courses in the latest technology. What about all the years he'd put in, all the classes he'd taken? No one ever praised him for that. It was just part of the job.

Even worse, the boss had never recommended these new high-tech classes. How was Bill supposed to know how important they were?

"One question," Bill said. "Can we get, you know, an update or review, summarizing what these classes covered? It might help all of us as a department."

The boss looked at Susan, one of the employees who had just finished the program.

"There was a lot of material," Susan said, "with lots of details. But maybe a few of us can put together a brief overview. Would that help?"

"Well," Bill said, "if we're going to need the details to do our jobs, maybe we should get them also." He turned toward the boss. "The rest of us will need this for our work, won't we?"

"Not at this point," the boss said. "You're really working on different projects. An overview should be enough."

Bill's face reddened. "From a team perspective, it just seems like we all ought to have the same information."

"'Team' means the coming together of different specialties," said Tom, another new employee. "We don't all have to know the same things."

"That's not entirely true," Bill said. "In fact, the history of work teams shows—"

His boss, looking frustrated, tabled the topic and went on to the next. At the end of the meeting, he pulled Bill aside.

"Look, Bill," he said. "What's all this nonsense about? If you want to take the class, why don't you just sign up for it?"

"That's a good idea," Bill said. "But I'm not sure I'll be able to with my workload the way it is."

Is Bill hinting that he wants to take the class? That he wants less work? That he feels left out or unappreciated? That he envies or resents the new employees? He clearly wants something, but he's not clear about what he wants.

Bill doesn't "own" his own needs, wants, or feelings. Instead, he leaves it up to others to figure out what he's after. This approach allows him to take the credit if an action works but *not* the responsibility if it doesn't. By acting as if the class is his boss's idea instead of his own, and by saying his workload is too much, Bill "can't lose"—if his performance declines, it's "the boss's fault" for "making" him take the class; if he doesn't take the class, it's "his boss's fault" for not lightening the workload; if he doesn't do well in class, it "was his boss's idea" in the first place.

If Bill refuses to own his goals and desires in an ordinary work situation, how might he act under intense pressure, when he feels angry or threatened? Very likely, he would refuse to admit how he feels, would blame others for his problems, would fail to acknowledge his own behaviors, and therefore would be unable to put limits on what he does. He easily could become violent *and claim that his victim provoked, "caused," or "asked for" the violence.* And he would believe it.

Bill clearly takes no control of his actions, has poor self-management skills, and shows no concern for his effect on others. His indirect manipulation is a high-risk behavior.

WITHDRAWAL AND RETRIBUTION

The employee withdraws, and later gets even, when things don't go his or her way, instead of directly telling others what he or she feels or wants.

Michelle had a lot at stake at today's supervisors' meeting. The manager had a reorganization plan and wanted all the supervisors to decide which way to go. The manager said she'd rather have the team decide than make the decision herself. What a cop-out, Michelle thought. What a way to make us hang ourselves. Or each other. She wanted things her way, so she hoped the others had the same ideas in mind.

"Let's start out," Michelle said at the meeting, "looking at how we're going to decide. What criteria should we use?" She wanted one of them to say something about the supervisors' own job security, so Michelle wouldn't have to say it.

Maybe some of them felt more secure about their jobs than she did. Maybe one or two actually believed that they'd come out okay even if their own employees were redistributed. Maybe they were so "in" politically they didn't have to worry. Maybe they were naive or stupid. Whatever it was, their reactions stunned her.

"I think we have to focus on the services needed and the skills required," said one recently hired supervisor. "I don't think we should put our individual needs ahead of the company's."

"We need to look at the clients," said a recently promoted supervisor. "It's supply and demand, according to what the clients want."

Michelle couldn't believe her ears. The other supervisors spent the rest of the meeting talking about surveying and interviewing the clients. Nothing about ways to make sure they all stayed on as supervisors. By now, Michelle hoped the manager would make the decision. It was bound to be better than what this group would come up with.

"Michelle, you haven't spoken since the start of the meeting," one of them said.

Michelle remained silent. She refused to comment, refused to vote, refused to commit herself to doing part of the survey. She avoided all of them for the next two weeks.

Two weeks later, when the manager asked for her candid input about the survey, Michelle said she appreciated the opportunity to talk to her.

"You've got a group of politicians, not supervisors," Michelle said. "I tried to focus on what's best from the client's viewpoint, but they're all just using this survey to prove how valuable they are to the firm. I don't want any part of that."

"Thanks," the manager said. "I'll keep that in mind."

Looking at behavior, Michelle's withdrawal and "getting even" is, in this example, more telling than her personal agenda or her lying. Although she had an agenda in mind, she said nothing about it and withdrew, and later retaliated, when none of them came up with her idea. Instead of saying she thought their ideas were unrealistic, she simply refused to take part. Later, when she tries to influence the manager, she gets even with her peers *without having told them what she wanted or that she was upset.*

Michelle's behavior goes two directions at once: "follow me—or else," as well as "guess where I'm going." No one can tell where she's going, and Michelle would claim it was *their* fault. She refuses to own her goals *or* her dissatisfaction, and instead focuses on revenge.

How far might she go when the pressure intensifies? Her retaliation easily could take the form of violence—unannounced and unacknowledged. Michelle does not take control of her actions, does not manage herself, and does not care how she affects those around her.

Michelle's tendency to withdraw and later get even is a high-risk behavior.

EXPECTATION OF FAILURE

The employee expects failure and lets it happen, instead of finding ways that would lead to success.

Ray knew he should have felt lucky to get this job. Getting fired from the last three jobs didn't help much when it came to looking for work. But he had a strong back and experience in construction, so this was the logical place to go. Besides, everyone in construction got fired from a job every now and then, and just started again on the next one. So they ought to give him a chance on this one.

Not that he expected it. No matter what your problem, no matter what you do or how hard you try, if the boss has it in for you, there's no way you'll make it. Take today, for example. Sure, it was the first day and maybe it's important to make a good first impression. But when he showed up half an hour late, the foreman just about chewed his head off. Ray explained about how he had to gather up his tools and then had trouble starting his truck, but the foreman didn't seem to care. He ordered Ray to "show your stuff" and make sure he was on time from now on. Ray glared at him, but that didn't change anything.

Well, Ray knew what that meant. This foreman didn't like him already, so what was the point of knocking himself out when it wasn't going to matter anyway. He'd had trouble with bosses like that before. They always wanted you to do things their way, but they never told you what that way was. Or if they did, and you tried, they picked on you anyway because they liked bossing everyone around. Ray knew this foreman was one of these bosses.

The next day he didn't show up at all. His arms and legs felt sore and he must have needed all that extra sleep. He woke up two hours after starting time, and he knew it didn't pay to show up late. He'd just wait until tomorrow.

When he showed up the next morning, he didn't bother to explain anything. He knew it wouldn't do any good. Sure enough, the foreman ran him off, saying he had no use for unreliable workers. Ray wasn't surprised. It just shows you that no matter how hard you try, no matter what you do, it won't work if bosses are against you.

Well, Ray'd had enough. If all those bosses thought they were too good to put up with a regular, decent worker, he'd show them a thing or two. Maybe even three or four, like the number of jobs he'd lost in a row.

He looked at all those tools and all that metal, workers walking on high beams, and the foreman chasing after all of them. Everyone quite a distance from their pickups–some of which, he noticed, had rifles in the back windows.

It shouldn't be too hard to prove his point.

More than simply blaming others, Ray clearly expects failure and takes *no* steps to prevent it–no alarm clock, no preparing his tools the night before, no clarification about work hours, no promises about getting himself together, no attempts to do it.

More than an "attitude" problem, Ray's *behaviors* make his negative expectations come true.

Ray's behavior is subtle and misleading. Because he does not *act* particularly upset or emotional, it would be easy to assume that he will leave quietly rather than seek revenge. However, the most telling thing about his behavior—silence, absence, tardiness, and unreliability—is what he's *not* doing: he is not talking, not arriving on time, not showing up at all, not being reliable. The only action he *does* take is to glare—silently. Ray's passive nonactions are negative ways he acts out his anger.

By the time you add the availability of weapons, the foreman's "fixed-target" position, the relative isolation of the site, and the fact that Ray has little to lose, you have a potentially lethal situation.

Ray clearly takes no control of his actions, has no self-management skills, and does not care how he affects those around him. His passive way of letting failure occur is a high-risk behavior.

When Mixed-Messenger employees act in passive-aggressive ways, you never know their real agendas, needs, feelings—or plans. Their unacknowledged anger makes them difficult to deal with.

All four passive-aggressive actions are high-risk behaviors.

Chapter 8

The Escape Artists:
Employees Who Avoid Reality

Most employees know the difference between reality and dreams, hopes, or fantasies. They may look forward to next year's vacation, wish they'd win the lottery, talk about the "dream" house they hope to have someday, picture how they'll live when they retire. But at the same time, they still deal with reality—the tasks, work assignments, meetings, deadlines, goals, relationships, plans, and general responsibilities that bring us back "down to earth."

Even though everyone has different *perceptions* or *interpretations* of something that happened, employees usually agree about *what* happened. They recognize the physical reality of events, even while acknowledging that their *reactions* to that reality may be different from someone else's. For most employees, fantasies serve as ways to release pressures caused by real life, and most employees know the difference between real life and fantasy. Even when they lie, *they* know the truth, despite what they choose to tell someone else.

High-risk employees try to *avoid* reality. As Escape Artists, they deny it, replace it, embellish it, and in general, substitute it with their own version. High-risk employees believe what they say, and they expect everyone else to believe them. Because they blend real-world facts with their own substitutions, it is hard to tell when they've gone from one to the other. Even worse, they can be so convinced–and convincing–about the "reality" of their substitutions that believing them is easy. Even after reality has shattered high-risk employees' presentation of "the facts," coworkers and managers easily can get duped into believing them again next time.

High-risk employees avoid reality in five ways.

ADDICTION

The employee relieves stress through using *addictive substances and/or activities*, instead of taking healthy steps to manage stress.

> Everybody loved Fridays, but Greg loved them more than anyone. He could hardly work on Fridays because his mind was elsewhere. Especially this weekend. His mind really would be "elsewhere" this weekend, because he had plans. All his organizational skills took on a new meaning when he planned for a weekend like this one.
>
> And he deserved it. Greg had worked six 12-hour days for the last eight months. Some of those weeks he'd worked all seven days, meaning he'd worked thirteen or twenty days in a row part of that time. If not for his buddies, he wouldn't have made it. They had what he needed so he could put in all those hours. Just the right amount gave him energy, a good feeling that all was well and he'd do fine. A little too much and he'd be nervous, jumpy, edgy, but still full of energy.
>
> They never noticed at work. He got so much done, more than any of his coworkers–probably more, in fact, than all of them combined. He did such good work, and so much, that nobody would question him. Plus he could go all shift long, and most of them couldn't. They got on his nerves more than usual, sometimes, but it was no big deal. The

company ought to be grateful for his buddies. If anyone really bugged him, he'd settle it with them in the parking lot. Maybe sooner. It depended on his mood. But so far, no one had messed with him.

It did make it tough to sleep, though. Many nights Greg could have stayed awake and then worked his next shift, but he knew he shouldn't. It was too dangerous, working with all those machines. He had to take good care of himself. Sure enough, his buddies helped out there, too. It just took a little to feel mellow, to get ready to lie down, and drift off. He owed all of that overtime money to his buddies' help. In fact, he had given a good portion of it to them already. He laughed when he thought about that.

Underneath his good mood Greg could feeling a hint of being drained, a buzzing kind of exhaustion. But at the same time he felt powerful, like mind over matter. Besides, he knew what to take to give him energy for this weekend. This weekend meant some real time off. He'd make up for all that responsibility and all those hours of work. Greg was going to party, with a capital "P."

Maybe he ought to take a little more right now. Three hours to go. Just a little bit would make the hours much shorter.

He needed a break anyway. In fact, he deserved it.

Whatever Greg is taking, it probably is some combination of illegal and dangerous. It also is seductive. On the surface, it appears to give Greg enough energy to work endlessly and probably even to do a good job for long periods of time, and it makes Greg feel as if he can handle the schedule. In the short run, it probably makes him feel good—and powerful. His substances give him the illusion that he is producing, that he's taking care of himself and that the situation is reasonable.

But it also makes Greg potentially dangerous to everyone at work. Physically, mentally, and emotionally exhausted from too much work, Greg uses the substances, instead of healthy steps, to reduce his stress. Ironically, the substances make his condition worse. His perceptions are off, his moods and feelings are likely to be unpredictable, his judgment probably is poor. If he's used substances for a while, they may have altered his brain chemistry in unpredictable ways. He could, at some point, become suspicious, paranoid, maybe even enough out of touch with reality to be called psychotic. Even if he uses the substances only outside of work, they still affect his brain, mind, and behavior wherever he is.

Greg and everyone around him at work are at the mercy of the chemical interaction among the substances, his brain, his personal history, his emotions, and his personality. Greg's illusion that he is fine—which his substances help create—makes him even more out of touch and more high-risk. What if he makes a mistake on the machinery and someone gets hurt? What if Greg gets angry at someone who "bugs" him? What has he got in his car that makes him want to go to the parking lot to "settle" things? Individuals' moods vary even under the best conditions. When you add drugs or alcohol, as well as exhaustion, it is hard to say what Greg might do.

Chapter 12 discusses addiction, and how it relates to employers and managers, in more detail. For now, it is enough to say that by being so out of touch with reality, Greg makes reality riskier for everyone. He clearly has no control over his own behavior, does not manage himself, and has no concerns about how he affects others. His use of addictive substances is a high-risk behavior.

DISTANCE FROM OTHERS

The employee *distances others*, instead of developing appropriate work relationships.

That stuff they said about being a better manager was out of bounds. Fred knew they hired him for his computer skills, and that's what he was going to give them. If they wanted a cheerleader for the job, they'd have to get a cheerleader type.

He'd already taught his employees more about programming than they'd learned in all the time they'd worked under his predecessor. What's more, he did it himself, instead of hiring an outside instructor, the way everyone else did. No one seemed to appreciate that. Even in today's performance review—the second one since he started here—he read very few comments about this fact or about all the costs he'd saved the firm by doing the training in the first place.

Instead, he read many comments such as "needs to be more customer-oriented," "still doesn't see enough of the big picture, including how his department affects marketing and production," and "needs improvement in being a team player." It reminded Fred a lot of report cards in grade school. So I don't "get along well with others," he thought to himself.

Frankly, he'd had enough. The real problem was that no one liked it when he told the truth. The marketing people would run over to him and expect him to do a rush job when they knew their deadline was two days earlier. They just wanted to blame him when they turned it in late. Fred told them so. And he also told them that if they'd watched out for the deadline in the first place, they wouldn't be in such a jam.

Production was another joke. They'd blame his programming when the real problem was their lack of attention to quality. Fred told them that also. He wasn't going to put up with all this nonsense just because the bosses didn't want to do their jobs. They used teams as an excuse not to keep things in line the way they should, and he'd told that to many a boss, every place he'd ever worked.

This review was just like all the others, everywhere he worked. As usual, Fred saw no reason to change. If they didn't like the way he was now, he knew how to make them wish he'd be like this again. All he had to do was get worse.

And he knew how. He'd done it before, and never gotten caught. He laughed to himself. He always made it look like an accident.

Both Fred's refusal to help and his negative criticism distance his coworkers when cooperative *work* relationships would be more appropriate. Note the emphasis on *work* relationships. If his coworkers complained because Fred wouldn't join them for lunch, joke around during work, or in some other way *socialize* more with them, Fred, as a private person, would have a right to say these demands were "out of bounds"–*for him*. Individuals have different preferences about privacy and involvement when it comes to socializing at work. But the actual complaints focused on Fred's refusal to *work* with his coworkers–making the complaints legitimate.

By distancing his coworkers instead of doing the necessary work, Fred fails to do his job–clearly a performance issue. But he also sets himself apart from everyone else. This separateness–especially because he also puts himself above the others–places Fred in a position to judge them and decide what they "deserve." With his history of poor reviews, followed by something that passes as accidents, revenge may be more a plan than a passing thought in Fred's mind.

He may or may not do something, and it may or may not be soon. But the clues are clear. Fred shows poor self-control, little self-management, and no concern for anyone, including the organization. His distancing is a high-risk behavior.

REALITY APPEARS BORING

The employee *finds reality too "flat" or boring*, instead of accepting the truth, finding real options, and working with them.

Jerry's coworkers described him as "versatile." It was a polite way of saying that his actions could go all over the map in one day–sometimes even in the same hour. In practical terms, they couldn't count on him. For example, he never did his paperwork, saying it was "too time-consuming," which made everyone else's jobs harder. But because he was the top salesperson for the third year in a row, they put up with whatever he did as if they had no opinions or feelings about it.

Last Monday, for example, he showed up frowning and scowling. As soon as he walked in, everyone knew to leave him alone. Usually, it just took a few good phone calls to cheer him up. Not this time. Jerry stayed the same until noon, when he locked up his office and said he'd be back by the end of the week. His coworkers knew he was headed for Las Vegas.

As soon as he showed up on Thursday, everyone knew Jerry had won. He was buoyant, visiting with everyone, asking how their families were doing, giving them pointers about certain customers. His mood lifted everyone else's. Everyone hated to admit it, but Jerry could be a lot of fun.

But by Friday, things changed again. Jerry even yelled at his secretary, something he'd done only once before. There were rumors that he once hit a secretary, when he worked at another firm. On Friday, when his secretary started crying, he went into his office and slammed the door shut. Noises of something cracking and breaking came from his office–maybe it was one of the models he had of the acrobatic planes he liked to fly. He was still there when everyone left that evening.

Right now, Jerry was on his way to see a customer. Everyone could tell because he left with that upbeat walk and optimistic smile. When he wanted to, Jerry could get along with, and impress, anyone. They'd know how the meeting went by how he acted when he came back.

Whether they wanted to know or not.

Jerry doesn't talk about what bothers him, take care of his paperwork, vent his stress through physical exercise, or professionally stick to business regardless of how he feels. Instead, he needs external stimuli before he can feel good, and he punishes everyone else with his bad moods. Even though we see no reference to drugs or alcohol, Jerry's sudden trips to Las Vegas and his quick and dramatic mood swings *may* signal addictive *behaviors* (which Chapter 12 discusses in more detail). His hobby of piloting small aerobatic planes could be seen as daredevil, "out-of-the-norm" behavior. Day-to-day reality, and appropriate steps to take to deal with it, appear too dull for Jerry.

So far, Jerry already has two negative effects on his coworkers: acting out his bad moods affects everyone; and even though his good moods are contagious, everyone else feels uneasy because of the roller coaster between his ups and downs. What if he loses all his money—or his car, or house—on his next trip to Vegas? What if his customers find out about his impulsive trips? Or if his employer catches on? Jerry clearly places no boundaries, or limits, on how much he acts out—or *takes* out—his feelings on others. Nor does he put boundaries between his *personal* feelings or circumstances and his *professional* role at work. Rumors that he once hit a secretary as well as the breaking noises coming from his office, give a glimpse of what he might do when he feels angry.

Jerry's volatile moods *and behaviors* show he has no self-control, cannot manage himself, and has no concern for his effect on others. His difficulty dealing with "flat and boring" reality is a high-risk behavior.

CREDIT IS EXAGGERATED
AND BLAME IS MINIMIZED

The employee *exaggerates credit and minimizes blame*, instead of taking appropriate credit and responsibility.

Everyone expected Pete to get the biggest bonus this year, even though they didn't think he really deserved it. He had such an uncanny knack for knowing when and how to get in the limelight that he even knew when to stay out of it. Just last fall, he refused to take part in a visible project that everyone else clamored to get in on. Later, when top management cut the project and laid off most of the employees assigned to it, everyone was convinced that Pete must have known something. But he never let on.

Then there was the meeting with the boss and several of her peers, where Pete made a great suggestion about how to improve the software. His coworkers had heard similar ideas from Don, a technical genius who didn't speak up much at meetings. But Pete claimed to have studied the problems and researched various options. The boss and her peers later referred to it as "Pete's idea," even though his teammates, at least, knew where it really came from.

Pete was a good team player—when it suited him. When the team had to redo part of a project because the numbers were wrong, Pete was the first to say "the team" had waited too long and "the team" didn't review the results thoroughly enough. He never mentioned that it was he who had run the data and given the results to the team. So far, no one dared challenge him. He had too much credibility with the bosses.

But rumor had it that a special investigation was underway—something about new-product information leaking to a competitive firm. They knew it had to be an employee, someone who, the rumor said, "had access to the data, was dishonest, but also was able to appear credible."

In addition to whatever *financial* harm Pete may have done to his employer, he also represents a *physical* risk if he fears getting—or if he gets—caught. Pete's behavior shows that instead of giving and taking appropriate credit and responsibility, he goes out of his way to look good *even if it means destroying others*. In normal competition, everyone tries to *be* or *do* the best. But Pete focuses on how he appears, rather than on how he really is or what he really does. His refusal to deal with reality and his dishonest ways of distorting reality to others make him potentially dangerous. Because he will not allow reality to crash through his fabricated world, Pete is at risk of trying to destroy others—literally—if he thinks they can expose the ways in which he has hurt his coworkers' or the company's future.

Because Pete already blames others, instead of owning responsibility for his actions, he easily may believe that others "set him up," whether he committed the crime or not. How far might he go if he thinks he has to defend or protect himself? Or if he tries to get even for what he thinks they did? Pete's defense and revenge may have no limits.

Pete's behavior shows that he has no self-control, poor self-management skills, and no concern for his coworkers or employer. His misrepresentations of credit and blame are high-risk behaviors.

DECEPTIVE BEHAVIOR

The employee lies and deceives others, instead of telling the truth.

Jack was stunned. He had kept out of it until Human Resources refused to back off. They kept complaining to him that Paula, who had started working for Jack three months ago, still had not produced verification for all her degrees. Because the job absolutely required the degrees, HR said Jack should never have put Paula on board without this verification. They wanted Paula's employment suspended until everything was cleared.

Jack felt lucky to have gotten Paula. She was on top of the latest technology, and also was a good team player—a combination few employees have. Clients liked Paula—she was smooth, professional, and credible. If Jack hadn't stepped in during the hiring mix-up and grabbed Paula, the competition would have gotten her. Even in the three months she'd been in Jack's department, Paul had proven her worth many times.

But Jack wanted to work with the system, so he kept checking with Paula. Paula kept saying she'd tried the university, she was working with HR to get to the right individual at the university, she'd gotten two or three different stories about what they thought happened to her records. "They clearly need the record-keeping software we use," Paula kept joking. But still no verification.

Jack wondered what he would have done next if circumstances hadn't changed because until yesterday, he really thought HR was getting in the way. But yesterday, without any warning at all, Paula showed up with a baseball bat and started swinging it. The secretary went to the hospital with a brain concussion, Paula's cube-mate got a broken shoulder and cracked ribs, and two other employees were still being diagnosed. Jack's arm was bruised from Paula grabbing at him as he helped the security guards.

Jack knew it had to be more than a coincidence, but he still couldn't see any connection between HR's insistence on sticking to the rules and Paula flipping out. He'd have to figure that out some time later.

Meanwhile, Jack wondered what would have happened to him if he'd been out in the open area with everyone else.

Maybe Paula knew she'd used her excuses for as long as she could. But the "connection" Jack tries to make between Human Resources' insistence on policy and Paula's unexpected violence is less direct than Jack would like. Whether Paula really had her degrees is not the main issue. The fact that she lied about it, and repeatedly embellished her lies, is the issue. Paula's "one lie" was a clue that *anything* could have been false. Maybe she never was as rational as she seemed. Maybe her "degrees" were not the only lies in her life. Maybe she was a spy for the competition. Maybe "Paula" was not her real name, the family photos on her desk were not her family, and she was wanted in another state for embezzlement or robbery or murder.

The problem with employees who lie and deceive is that you can't tell what's real. You can't even assume you—or anyone—will be safe with them. Because liars sometimes get caught up in their own fabrications, it's even hard to tell what *they* think is real. *Anything* is possible with an employee who lies.

Even before she became violent, Paula's behavior showed she has no control over her actions, no self-management, and no concerns for how she affects anyone else. Paula's tendency to lie and deceive is a high-risk behavior.

When you deal with Escape Artist employees, you can't tell what they really need or feel—or might do. And because they work hard at avoiding reality, it's hard to hold them accountable.

All five ways of avoiding reality are high-risk behaviors.

Chapter 9

The Shockers:
Employees Whose Behaviors
Change Suddenly, Dramatically,
and/or for the Worse

At work, most employees do a good job and continue to do so over time. They maintain their high level of quality, meet deadlines, ask questions, and generally act in dependable ways. In addition to their specific work performance, quality employees usually act in other reasonable, predictable ways: they get along with their coworkers, dress appropriately, take care of their health and hygiene, generally act calm and cheerful, have relatively stable moods, and behave consistently. Even as they learn new skills and adapt to changes, most employees stay "themselves."

Yet, under a number of conditions, even reliable employees may become high-risk–sometimes, very suddenly. These Shockers change in ways that catch managers unprepared. Behaviors you have learned to expect, to take for granted, and to count on suddenly are replaced by unreliable, negative, and sometimes even frightening behaviors.

Healthy, normal changes occur over relatively long periods of time–the trainee who develops expertise, the computer-phobe who learns to love technology, the poor performer whose skills improve through training. However, with high-risk employees, the change is sudden, dramatic, and usually–although not always–for the worse. For managers, timing makes an important difference when dealing with the Shockers.

Reliable employees may become high-risk in eight different ways.

DEPRESSION TURNS TO HAPPINESS

A depressed employee *suddenly appears happy*, instead of recovering in small steps over a period of time.

> Ty hadn't taken the news well at all. When his manager tried to explain that he'd restructured the department to make it easier to get input from customers, Ty listened politely but said he still felt as if he'd been "put out to pasture" now that a new supervisor had been put between him and his manager. Nothing the manager said could change Ty's mind.
>
> For the three months since then, he'd acted detached and remote. He kept his office door closed, said nothing at meetings, looked at no one. His posture slumped, making him look shorter than he was. Ty looked "caved in" and defeated. He still did a good job in his technical work, but his people skills had fallen to zero. When Ruth, his new supervisor, tried to talk to him, he listened but simply refused to answer. When Ruth suggested that he talk to someone in Human Resources or the Employee Assistance Program, Ty simply said it wasn't necessary. Ruth didn't want to force anything, but if Ty didn't cheer up by performance appraisal time, she'd have to take some action then.
>
> Everyone was surprised one morning when Ty walked in smiling, and greeted everyone. He looked and acted like his old self, standing tall, with color in his face and plenty of energy. Ruth felt relieved but said nothing. The manager walked into Ty's office, which Ty had kept open.

"Good morning," the manager said. "Looks like you're feeling better."

"A lot better," Ty said. "A whole lot."

"Well, good. Let me know if I can do anything."

When the manager went home that evening, he found that someone had broken in through the back door, shattered the glassware, ransacked all the drawers, and smashed all the furniture with an ax. Nothing was missing.

When the police arrived, they noted that it didn't look like a burglary. They asked the manager if he knew anyone who might have a personal grudge against him.

Although most managers and coworkers would assume Ty really felt better, his "recovery" was too sudden to be true. His cheerfulness may have made more sense if it were seen as the pleasure he got from revenge.

In a real recovery from three months of job-related depression, Ty would have become his old self in smaller steps over a longer period of time. He might have told his manager that he was working on accepting the change, even though he still didn't like it. He might have told Ruth he resented feeling downgraded but he didn't blame her personally. He might have talked a little bit with his coworkers or at meetings. In a real recovery, Ty would have emerged from his depression by making small positive gestures, not uniformly nor consistently, but erratically and slowly. Ty's sudden cheerfulness did not mean what it appeared to mean.

Sometimes, depressed employees who "recover" too suddenly are at risk of hurting *themselves*, as well as others. Chapter 11 will go into more detail about this process.

For Ty's manager, the "recovery" was a warning sign. Superficially "his old self," Ty still did not show any self-control, self-management, or real concern for others. The suddenness with which he acted happy is a high-risk behavior.

SUDDEN WITHDRAWAL OR DEPRESSION

A generally content employee suddenly appears *withdrawn or depressed*, especially if outward circumstances have not changed, *but even if they have.*

Ralph, who had been his manager, spent a lot of time thinking about Ed. Ed usually kept to himself, but so did Ralph and just about everyone else in the computer room. Ed got along all right with his coworkers, had a performance history of average and above-average ratings, and never had created any problems. The only thing Ralph could think of that made Ed different was that his wife and stepdaughter were from France, but even that didn't seem like much.

Ralph also had trouble figuring out when Ed might have shown signs of being in trouble, maybe backing off more or showing less interest in work. Ed was so private all the time, it was hard to tell. Maybe it started about the same time as rumors about layoffs. There'd been a layoff a year earlier, and rumors about another one had started a few months ago. Ralph wondered. Ed had taken one day off around that time, which was unusual for him. He might have been a little quieter at meetings, too. One time, in fact, he appeared not to have heard a question directed at him, and later he said he'd been having problems with his ears. Ralph had believed what Ed said. How was he supposed to know what to look for, especially in such a quiet employee?

Ralph felt his face heat up. He hated to admit it, but on top of everything else, he felt angry. He'd already come to terms with his shock about the event, his sorrow for the family, and even his own guilt for not noticing any symptoms. But Ralph knew it would take a while for him to accept his anger.

Last Saturday, Ed had locked himself in his bedroom and shot himself in the head. He'd left a note blaming "Ralph and the rest of the managers" at work, saying they "threatened my security."

Suicide may not, at first glance, appear dangerous to anyone besides the victim and his or her survivors. But, as Chapter 11 discusses in more detail, suicide and murder are two sides of the same coin. Because Ed's anger stayed inward, or imploded, when he reached the level of desperation associated with both suicide and murder, he took it out on himself. But if at that point of desperation his anger had gone outward, or exploded—toward, for example, Ralph or another manager—Ed might just as easily have committed murder. At this level of desperation, the possibility exists—for an unspecified time preceding the actual event—that the employee will commit *either* suicide *or* murder *or both*. Shortly before Ed killed himself, Ralph was in just as much danger as Ed.

As Ralph noted, Ed exhibited symptoms so subtle that Ralph didn't notice them at the time. In a more outgoing employee, withdrawal or depression would have stood out more dramatically. With low-key, even-tempered employees, managers have to pay more attention to detail and look more closely than usual. It may have helped if Ralph had known to ask Ed, "How are you doing? Have you heard rumors about layoffs? How do you interpret them? It seemed to me that you were down during this meeting—is that the case?" Whether Ed answered honestly or not, his manner and tone could have given Ralph a better chance to read Ed's moods—*if* Ralph had known what to look for.

The rumors about layoffs created negative *external* circumstances—conditions that could affect anyone. For managers, external circumstances—such as layoffs, mergers, reorganization, and other changes at work—make a logical starting point in noting *who* might feel vulnerable or angry at any given time and *when* employees might be susceptible to these feelings.

But even when no external circumstances call for caution, you still must focus carefully on employees' behavior. As also may

have been true of Ed, personal problems–*internal* circumstances–may be driving them. If you know about an employee's
personal circumstances, such as a pending divorce or health
problems, you can be more alert to the employee's susceptibility.

By the time he committed suicide, Ed clearly had become
dangerous. Before that, his retreating actions–mild though they
looked–showed he was losing control, was unable to manage
himself, and was losing interest in others. Ed's withdrawal and
depression were high-risk behaviors.

PERFORMANCE SUDDENLY DECLINES

The work performance of a good employee *suddenly declines*,
whether or not circumstances could account for the change.

> As the controller, Phil was as professional as they come. He
> focused on the numbers and the bottom line and stayed out
> of personality conflicts. He also did small things that
> pleased his peers, such as sending them articles he thought
> would interest them. A Vietnam veteran, Phil had a solid,
> disciplined way about him.
>
> But a few days ago, Jim, the vice president to whom Phil
> reported, was surprised to find a few minor errors in Phil's
> numbers. He also noticed that one of Phil's reports was not
> in yet, and it was unusual for Phil to be late. Later that day,
> Jim overheard someone say that Phil "was in the first bad
> mood I've ever seen him in–and I've been here five years.
> He actually told someone off at that meeting."
>
> Jim couldn't think of any problems that started a few
> days ago. If anything, he'd told Phil some good news–that
> Phil finally could hire the assistant controller he'd needed.
> Jim remembered that Phil's reaction was less enthusiastic
> than Jim had expected. Jim figured it didn't mean anything.
> Still, he wondered what was going on with Phil.

When he asked, Phil simply brushed it off. "A few things caught up with me all at once," Phil said, "but I've got everything back under control now."

Several days later, Jim again found some errors in Phil's calculations. Phil's whole manner struck him as detached or distracted and, sometimes, even rude. Again, Jim asked what was happening and again Phil brushed him off.

For some reason, Jim wasn't too surprised when the new assistant controller walked in and said, "Can we talk? I've got some important information for you."

He was surprised when the assistant said, "I know this sounds crazy. But when I told Phil some of the balances were off, he mumbled something that sounded a lot like 'blow up your car.' When I asked him to repeat himself, he said, 'Nothing, I was only joking.' But I'm scared. What do you know about him?"

Obviously, Jim knew a lot less about Phil than he thought. As Chapter 10 describes in more detail, managers cannot possibly know "enough"–about potentially dangerous behavior *or* about each employee's personal issues–to tell whether an employee has gone over the edge or simply is having a bad work day. Like any manager, all Jim had observed was the way Phil *behaved*. Jim tried to ask Phil what was happening, but he was too easygoing and accepting when Phil brushed him off. Jim would have been ahead if he'd interpreted the brush-off as an additional problem behavior and insisted that Phil explain things more thoroughly.

Although any decline in performance means problems exist, a *sudden* decline usually means that the employee has become overwhelmed by the emotional aspect of the problem. This exaggerated emotional component makes the problem more volatile, unpredictable, and potentially dangerous.

Maybe Phil had embezzled money, and he feared that an assistant would expose him. Maybe he suffered from Vietnam flashbacks, and the timing just happened to coincide with the hiring of the assistant. Maybe Phil had personal problems that affected, but did not come from, work. By emphasizing Phil's sudden decline in performance and in professional behavior, and by insisting on a deeper conversation about both, Jim may have found out, in a general sense, that Phil had personal problems and needed help. The in-depth conversation also may have brought to the surface the fact that Jim had better examine the books—*and* that Phil was potentially dangerous. Whether or not he could think of external circumstances that might "explain" the change in Phil's behavior, Jim needed to pursue the issue further than he did.

Phil clearly was losing control of his actions, failing to manage himself, and losing concern for how he affected others. His sudden decline in performance was a high-risk behavior.

SUDDEN ATTENDANCE PROBLEMS

The *attendance* of a reliable employee suddenly becomes erratic, whether or not circumstances could account for the change.

Juan was so dependable that his supervisor often had him train new employees. He always emptied the boxes and stocked the shelves energetically, and cleaned up carefully. Best of all, he always showed up on time and was a good role model for everyone.

So the store manager was surprised when Juan showed up late for one shift.

"Hey, I apologize," Juan said quickly. "I had to take care of a problem at home, but I didn't think I'd be late."

"Thanks, I understand," the manager said. "No problem."

But the second time he was late that week, the manager became concerned. He noticed that Juan was a little sloppy about the shelves. "Can I help out in some way?" he asked Juan. "Do you need some time off?"

"No, no, I can't afford it," Juan said. "Look, I really apologize. It won't happen again." During the shift, the manager noticed that Juan moved more slowly than usual and seemed distracted.

When Juan missed the next shift completely, the manager called his house. "I'm worried about you, man," he said. "What's going on?"

"I'm sick," Juan said. "I'm really, really sorry. I meant to call you earlier, but I've been sleeping. I promise I'll be there tomorrow."

It was too late to call anyone else to work the shift, but the manager tried anyway. After three no-answers, he did some of the stocking himself.

On Saturday, when he was ready to schedule for the next week, the manager wondered about Juan. He put him on his usual schedule, but he also arranged for an extra worker to be on those shifts, just in case. The manager couldn't afford to do that for long, but Juan had been so reliable that the manager wanted to help all he could. Maybe Juan had some personal problems at home. Maybe he was sick and too embarrassed to admit he felt too weak to work.

That evening, right before closing time, a young man walked in and asked for Juan, saying he was Juan's brother.

"He's home sick," the manager said. "You ought to know about that if you're his brother."

"Well, let's just say I don't. See, Juan owes me a bunch of money," the stranger said.

"You'll have to take that up with Juan. We're closing now." The manager gestured toward the door.

The stranger pulled out a pistol. "Stop right there," he said. "You'll just have to take care of Juan's debt for him."

If Juan took part "behind the scenes," he clearly caused the dangerous situation. If not, the danger still came *indirectly* from him, through his "brother," and any information he innocently may have given the man. In either case, Juan's sudden unreliability signaled that something had changed for the worse. When Juan's attendance remained a problem *even after* the manager tried to find out what was wrong and offered to help, it became a warning sign that, unfortunately, the manager did not read.

If Juan had a job-related problem, the manager gave him plenty of room to say so. By guessing that it was a personal or health problem–that is, by blaming circumstances, especially when the circumstances are in the manager's own mind–the manager unwittingly "explained away" the problem when he should have emphasized that the attendance problem was unacceptable. For example, *not* scheduling Juan for a week may have made a better point than scheduling an "extra" for Juan's shift.

If the manager had guessed that the problem involved drug use, he may have made a different decision. But managers should not have to–and really are not qualified to–guess accurately. A useful guideline for managers is that they must deal *only with the behaviors, especially if the behaviors are worse*, instead of guessing the cause. As Chapter 11 will show you, so many possible causes exist for high-risk behaviors that managers must focus on the *behaviors*–regardless of what they think is the cause. Even if they know the circumstances or causes, the problem behavior at work still must be resolved.

Juan's sudden and negative change in reliability showed that he was losing control of his actions, losing his skill in self-management, and was less concerned about how he affected others. His sudden erratic attendance was a high-risk behavior.

ACTION IS OUT OF CHARACTER

An employee does something *out of character*, especially if it is dramatic or extreme.

Bud was a family man. Photos of his wife and kids covered his desk, and every Monday he went on and on about the kids' soccer, or baseball, or swimming. He looked genuinely happy when he talked about his wife or kids. Married ten years, his coworkers nicknamed him "The Newlywed."

So his manager was surprised one Monday to hear that on the previous Friday, after work, someone saw Bud at an out-of-the way restaurant with Debbie from marketing. The manager assumed it was business-related—maybe Bud was helping Debbie work with a client—although the manager admitted that was pretty unlikely.

The following week, the manager overheard three employees talking about Bud.

"I thought it was just Debbie," one said, "so I was shocked to hear he was there with Ann."

"Talk about midlife crisis!" the second employee said.

"Watch out, he'll be asking you out next," the third one said.

More curious than worried, the manager started watching Bud a little more closely. Sure enough, he made fewer comments about his wife and kids. Within two more weeks, he spoke about them only when someone asked him a question.

One evening, when everyone had left, the manager looked inside Bud's office to see if the family pictures still dominated his desk. They did. The manager looked inside the top drawer. Maybe there'd be pictures of someone else.

In an unsealed envelope in the back of the drawer, the manager saw some powder and four pills. Time to check with Human Resources, the manager thought. Better see if my snooping was legal.

Some people may consider Bud's behavior "normal" or at least "common." Even beyond personal values or morals, Bud may be going through a midlife crisis, a problem with drugs or alcohol, or problems related to his brain chemistry or general health. Chapter 11 discusses in detail the issue of possible causes.

For now, once again, the manager has to focus on *what Bud does*, rather than on why.

The changes in Bud's behavior are different enough to indicate a problem. Because Bud acts so out of character, assumptions anyone has made about him no longer apply. As with so many other high-risk employees, no one can predict what he will–or won't–do. If Bud handles cash, can the manager still assume Bud is honest? If Bud knows that his coworkers found out about his affairs, can anyone be sure Bud will react calmly and reasonably? What would happen if someone tells Bud's wife? How likely is it that Bud uses drugs at work? Even if the "powder and pills" turn out to be illicit drugs or illegally used prescription medicine, they present only *an additional* potential danger at work. Bud's unpredictability remains the biggest risk.

Bud is losing the control he used to have over his actions, and he neither manages himself nor shows concern for his effect on others. Bud's out of character behaviors are high-risk.

EXTREME OR DANGEROUS BEHAVIOR

An employee does *anything extreme or inherently dangerous*, even if it is something he or she "has always done."

> Chuck had been an ironworker for years, but he never paid enough attention to the safety rules. In the old days, when he first started, everyone was pretty casual about safety issues. But as times changed and safety became more important on the job, Chuck refused to go along with all the rules. For example, although he wore his safety belt, he had disabled the safety latch on the hook. He had wired the latch open, so it couldn't spring shut as it was designed to do. Too much trouble, Chuck had complained. He overlooked too many safety rules for the same reason. His foreman, Les, got tired of following Chuck around all day and chewing him out.

Early this morning, Chuck hung by his safety belt on the curtain of reinforcing steel that later would be embedded in a concrete wall. When he had to move from one part of the steel curtain to another, he unhooked his safety hook and, moving hand over hand, climbed twenty feet across to his next work spot. Out of habit, Chuck casually attached his hook to a steel bar and let go, freeing his hands for work. The hook, its safety latch wired open, slipped off the bar. Chuck fell thirty feet to the concrete deck.

The pipefitter upon whom he fell also died.

So far in this chapter, the employees' performance started at a high level and then declined. With Chuck, however, several of his *typical, regular* behaviors are high-risk. Day-to-day, his foreman clearly had tried, unsuccessfully, to get Chuck to comply with safety regulations.

Employees like Chuck put managers in a bind. These employees often are both experienced and good at what they do, which makes it hard for managers to "hassle" them about rules. Even though these employees clearly endanger both themselves and others, it often takes a tragedy to prove the wisdom of the rules. Les, Chuck's foreman, may have looked foolish if he'd refused to let Chuck work on the steel curtain—even though this is exactly what he should have done. Chapter 11 describes ways to deal with problem behaviors.

Chuck *often* lost control of his actions, actively took steps *not* to manage himself, and clearly put others at risk. His ongoing behavior was high-risk.

HIGH-RISK EMPLOYEE IS FIRED

An employee who exhibits high-risk behaviors is fired, even if he or she is fired for reasons *other than* these behaviors.

As her new manager, Andy had no idea this would happen. He knew Betty was having problems in her new job, and working for him, but he'd never expected it to come to this.

Andy had started out trying to help Betty, saying things like, "You're learning quickly. Here's a shortcut to make this step a little easier." Betty never seemed particularly receptive, but she didn't seem hostile, either. Andy was used to this quiet resistance, especially from individuals like Betty who knew they needed to learn but didn't like to admit it. As a pioneer of sorts in her day, Betty was one of the few women who focused her life almost solely on her career. Yet as obsessed as she was with her job, Betty always resisted new technology and new ways of working.

But after a while, Betty got sullen whenever Andy tried to show her something. Andy began to wonder whether Betty really just didn't want to learn.

By the time Andy had to start documenting performance problems, he was convinced Betty didn't care about her job. She showed up late, got into conflicts regularly with everyone on her team, sulked when anyone made a suggestion, repeatedly made the same mistakes and blamed everyone else for them. One time, Andy thought he smelled alcohol on Betty's breath, but he wasn't sure. Andy also noticed that Betty was a loner. She never took coffee breaks and she ate lunch alone.

By the time Andy needed to give Betty her performance review, he had what should have been enough documentation to let her go. But because she had worked there so long, and had gotten good reviews from bosses to whom she'd made it clear that work was the center of her life, Andy's would be her first negative review. So he got people from Human Resources to help him.

Andy tried to make it easy for Betty.

"It's nothing personal about you," Andy said. "It's just that the fit's no longer any good. Your work was fine under different conditions, but now a lot of things have changed. You'll probably do better at a place where you can work more on your own. Our new emphasis on teams just isn't for everyone."

Betty said nothing, Andy remembered. She just got up, grabbed her purse, and walked out. In a way, this made it easier than Andy had expected.

Three days later, Andy was out on the floor helping one of his employees with the machines. He was shocked when Betty showed up and walked rapidly down the hall.

Everyone heard the repeated explosions as Betty opened fire, into each office, with what the police later identified as a 9mm handgun.

Betty presented two kinds of problems for Andy—poor performance of the technical skills needed to do the job and high-risk behaviors. Andy's documentation and reasons for firing her emphasized only the *performance* problems, using objective data instead of what could sound like personal biases. Andy behaved *reasonably.*

But the high-risk behaviors—distancing others, acting out her anger instead of talking about it, repeating the same mistakes, passive-aggressively "refusing" to learn or cooperate, possibly using alcohol at work, and her obsession with her job—showed that Betty was *not reasonable.* The company's performance review system may not have allowed Andy to discipline Betty for these behaviors, but Andy could have used them as warning signs—*if he had known how to read them.* Chapter 11 describes options Andy could have used.

Most violence from fired employees occurs within one week after the firing (Berry, 1994). Had the manager known how to recognize high-risk behaviors, he might have had more options about firing Betty–and, perhaps, even about having her work for him. When high-risk employees are fired, the risk may become even greater.

EMPLOYEE IS ABUSED OUTSIDE OF WORK

The employee is mistreated by his or her *spouse*, especially if the spouse's behavior fits any of the high-risk descriptions.

Walt knew the halls and walkways almost as well as if he worked there. Polly's employer allowed family visitors, and Walt had been there a lot.

No one thought much about it when he walked in. They knew who he was. No one knew the rage he felt. Or that Polly had moved to another apartment last night because she was tired of the bruises, always on the parts of her body that were covered when she dressed for work, so no one could tell. Tired of the nights he didn't show up at home, the nights he sat there drinking steadily. Tired of asking, begging him to change. Tired of his promises. It kept getting harder to keep up the cheerful smile and peppy voice at work. She left to save her life.

He was furious about it. She had no business even showing up early at work and staying late, much less leaving him. She probably had a lover at work, which explained all the so-called overtime she put in. "Total Quality Teams" my ass, he thought. No one knew he had something to prove to her, how much he wanted her to be his, how much she had to be his and no one else's. She had no business leaving him. He'd show her.

No one knew how long he had collected guns, how many were in his apartment, how many hours he'd spent on target practice.

No one knew how long the barrel was on the pistol hidden in his jacket.

Employees' family and personal problems create blind spots for managers, because it's hard to tell when the problems will spill over into the workplace. Walt may very well shoot Polly at work. If his aim is a little off, he may accidentally hit the person at the next desk. If Polly is gone from her desk, Walt may decide to shoot her "lover"–that is, whichever coworker (or manager) matches his fantasy. If Polly is gone for the day and Walt goes berserk, he may no longer care *whom* he shoots. And if he shoots anyone, Polly's coworkers be will be traumatized by the event.

Even if Polly had told her manager or coworkers what was going on, they probably would not have known what to do. Any preventive steps they took may have meant working in constant fear; trying to tell whether Walt was dangerous at this specific moment and, possibly, depriving him of his constitutional rights if he were searched because of hearsay–especially in an open environment he'd visited many times before.

Many organizations invite employees' family members to visit and see where the spouse or parent works. But this friendly gesture has a down side when family problems–and high-risk ways of dealing with them–carry over into the workplace.

Worst of all, the manager had no way of knowing that Walt was a high-risk person. Polly, not the manager, saw Walt when he acted out his anger, blamed her for his problems, acted impulsively, sought immediate gratification (in venting his anger), overreacted, "got even" without acknowledging his problems, and had outbursts of rage. Only Polly knew that Walt saw no relationship between how he treated Polly and what the consequences would be, repeated the same mistakes, had an infant-like awareness only of himself, tried to control her, saw events as fragmented, and relieved stress through substance abuse. Even if the manager knew, there still was no way to predict what today's visit would mean. By the time Walt showed up, he'd gone past high-risk and was dangerous.

From the manager's point of view, Polly is a high-risk employee because of her *spouse's* high-risk behaviors. Chapter 11 will discuss ways to deal with these situations.

By definition, the Shockers' actions catch managers off guard. The negative behaviors may be small enough to excuse, may not be directly related to danger, or may be so familiar that they are hard to recognize.

But they're still dangerous.

REFERENCE

Berry, K. M., "How to Protect Your Company from Office Violence," *Investor's Business Daily*, March 28, 1994, p. 4.

Chapter 10

The Strangers:
Employees Who Behave in Remote or Withdrawn Ways

Among the high-risk employees described so far, you've seen outward behaviors that fit, or at least *appeared* to fit, within the normal range—that is, until a crisis occurred. They suffer from problems that are emotional and/or mental *but which are not immediately visible*. Their normalcy contributes to the trouble you have identifying a problem soon enough.

But the Strangers present an entirely different scenario, *even in the absence of external pressures*. Their *usual* behavior is unusual enough, and sometimes even bizarre enough, to make you marvel at their ability to get any work done or even to show up at all. The Strangers may talk to themselves, appear mildly unkempt to downright unwashed, make unusual facial expressions or hand gestures, or sit in strange positions. They may act out an emotion that is totally out of place—such as laughing when something sad occurs at work, getting angry when someone announces good news, or crying when nothing external occurs. The Strangers may express bizarre beliefs, such as believing spies or space aliens work in the same building or follow them home, or magical thinking, such as believing people physically put thoughts into their heads. They may take your comments so literally that you think they are making fun of you. For example:

- If you ask, "What brings you to talk to me?"
- and you expect an answer such as, "I'm having some work problems I thought you could help me with" or "I needed some information,"
- the Stranger may say, instead, "I usually take the elevator."

The Strangers also may fail to respond when you make a joke. Their demeanor may be withdrawn and emotionally flat all the time, or most of the time but with occasional–and extremely forceful–outbursts.

Chapter 11 describes in detail why you *absolutely cannot and must not* "diagnose" your employees. The general point is that *numerous* conditions can create *any* of the high-risk behaviors, including those enacted by the Strangers. Nevertheless, as a manager, you need to be aware that unlike the other high-risk employees, *the Strangers probably suffer from some form of psychosis*, of which all the behaviors described above *may* be symptoms. You must recognize this possibility *because it increases the risk to you and your employees*, as described below.

The Americans with Disabilities Act includes mental illness and–although any exact interpretations and limits have yet to be determined–you face a greater chance now than in the past that one or more of your employees suffer from *some form* of mental illness, including the possibility of psychosis. It also is important to note that, so far, we have *assumed* the other high-risk employees were "normal"–and many "normal" employees are capable of performing high-risk behaviors–but the possibility always exists that they are not. This paradox comes from the inherent and eternal difficulty of defining "normal" and "abnormal"–and of distinguishing between them (Robbins, 1993).

Psychosis is a severe form of mental illness in which *at least some of the time*–but *not necessarily all the time*–the individual's thinking processes and five physical senses function in distorted ways. While in a psychotic state, the Stranger may "hear" voices that no one else hears and "see" people or events that no one else sees. Sometimes they may hallucinate odors, tastes, or physical sensations. Even when they are *not* hallucinating, psychotics tend to think in unusual or magical ways. They also tend to be extremely concrete, interpreting what you say very literally. They neither initiate nor understand humorous comments. The most common form of psychosis is schizophrenia, although experts disagree about the exact nature of this mental illness (Robbins, 1993). Individuals suffering from extreme forms of bipolar disorder (formerly called manic-depression) and severe clinical depression also may have psychotic episodes.

Unlike stereotyped images, which portray psychosis as an around-the-clock condition, most psychotics move in and out of psychotic states, and to varying degrees at different times. They hallucinate only some of the time, and even while hallucinating, they still may function and interact in what most people know as the "real world." *They may be good workers, especially in jobs that are highly structured and which produce tangible results.* But even then, the Strangers are likely to exhibit unusual behaviors and to have problems getting along with their coworkers. In addition to the behaviors described above, psychotics cannot deal with stress—under stress, they will "decompensate" by becoming either extremely forceful or more withdrawn. Many Strangers are reclusive, nearly unnoticeable employees who perform adequately in jobs that are routine and repetitive and which have relatively predictable outcomes. As long as the Strangers are quiet and productive, you may never be able to—nor need to—recognize that they are psychotic.

But the problem is that *occasionally, their extreme forcefulness can turn into outbursts of rage.* As a manager, you must be able to tell when their unusual behavior is still *functional* and when it is *high-risk.*

The Strangers go from unusual to high-risk behaviors in five ways.

OBSESSION WITH PLANS

The *obsessive* employee comes up with "explanations" or "plans."

> Wayne knew a lot about guns. In the twenty-five years he'd worked there, he taught dozens, maybe hundreds, of co-workers just about everything they needed to know about hunting, target-practice, rifles, pistols, shotguns, semi-automatics, even home and personal security. Wayne loved guns, and as he always said, he had a lot of respect for what they could do.
>
> Sometimes Wayne got carried away. He'd get off the subject of hunting and get into his thing about the military, how only the military knew how to run things, how the military was the ultimate of freedom because it kept you safe, how being in the military was the biggest honor. When anyone asked him which service he'd been in, Wayne always got an odd look on his face, shook his head and said, "It's too much. Another time." Then he'd change the subject. No one had ever been to his house, but the rumor was that it looked like an armory.
>
> So no one was surprised when Wayne started talking about how a better military could "solve all the problems we've got, here at work, in the whole city, even the whole world. Too many dangerous people around."
>
> "The Guard, the Army, none of them are doing the job," Wayne went on. "We need our own militia. Check the people who show up at work here. Check who's going in and out of banks. Check your house, your garage, airports. Everywhere," Wayne said. "They're not going to solve the problems, we'll have to do it ourselves. I'll have all the plans finished up real soon."
>
> Only a few were surprised when he showed up at work one day in camouflage clothes with a hand-made insignia

on his shirtsleeve. "I'm organizing right now," he said. "You want to join, you come sign up. I got the list right here."

The next day, when the building had to be evacuated because of an anonymous call about a "mass murder," everyone knew who the most likely suspect was.

Wayne *may or may not* be psychotic, but his *behavior—not* the cause or condition leading to it—is your focus as a manager. Even before he started "organizing," Wayne behaved in strange ways. His obsession with guns made him a fanatic. Whether an obsession focuses on guns, knives, political parties or philosophies, cults, military organizations, religion, religious rituals, racial superiority, "get-rich-quick" schemes, drugs, *or anything else*, the obsessive quality itself is strange and high-risk.

Wayne's obsession was easy to miss *as a high-risk behavior* because his knowledge was helpful. In the traditional male culture, guns fit the macho image—an image discussed in more detail in Chapter 12. Wayne could appear to be "one of the boys" when he talked about guns. That fine line between "normal" and "fanatic" is hard to pinpoint—but it was clear, by the time Wayne showed up in camouflage and tried to sign people up, that he had crossed it.

As soon as Wayne combined his obsession with explanations of what was wrong with the world and "plans" to solve it, his behavior became high-risk.

ONE COWORKER IS TARGETED

The *generally suspicious employee* focuses on a specific coworker, manager, or customer.

Bill made it clear from his first day on the job that he had no use for most people, because, "You never know when they'll take advantage of you." Everyone agreed that at least he was honest about it, and consistent. Bill didn't trust anything any of them did. He'd ask two others before believing what the first coworker told him, or he'd add the numbers himself to make sure they got it right.

Throughout the day, he'd sometimes move his lips a lot, as if he were talking to himself. When a coworker asked him about it, he said, "This is between me and someone else. It's none of your business." On top of that, he smelled bad. When the boss discreetly said something about him needing a shower, Bill said the smell "keeps me safe from people." They were pretty sure he didn't even mean it as a joke.

So Bill was pretty hard to put up with from the start. But now he was even worse. He started blaming Alice for his mistakes, claiming she was "breaking up the thoughts" inside his head.

"You do it with your eyes," he said. "Quit looking at me." Alice gladly turned her desk around to face another direction.

Then he accused Alice of stealing his ideas. At first, it sounded as if he thought she'd rummaged through his desk. But he made it very clear when he said, "Alice puts her thoughts into my head. They gather up my ideas. When she takes her thoughts out, my ideas go with them."

Alice told the boss she was so afraid of Bill that she couldn't come to work. The boss didn't know what to say.

He was just as afraid.

Even though Bill's earlier behaviors were strange and annoying, they were relatively harmless. His coworkers felt uncomfortable with him and disliked him, but he apparently did his work.

Yet as soon as his suspicion focused on one employee, he became high-risk, for several reasons:

1. That employee–in this case, Alice–becomes the single target for his generalized suspicion. This means that now *all* his suspicions, energies, *and delusions* will focus on her. She is at serious risk.
2. Because Bill loses touch with reality, and operates in his own private and isolated version of it, it is impossible for his boss or coworkers to know *what he thinks is happening.* Because he believes what he says about Alice, he may think he has to protect or defend himself, or punish her or . . . who knows?
3. Once Bill has gone this far outside reality and into his own world, there is no way to tell what he will do. He may see *all* his coworkers as out to get him, or the boss as a spy watching him. He may hallucinate everyone pointing guns at him. The most dangerous thing about Bill is that *whatever he does will make sense to him, based on his own perception of reality*–and no one else knows what that is or what he will do. Once he goes this far, his "logic" is different from everyone else's.

By the time Bill accused Alice of literally stealing ideas from his head, the manager finally recognized that Bill was high-risk. But the first clue actually occurred earlier, when Bill complained about Alice's eyes breaking up his thoughts. The minute Bill singled out one individual, he was high-risk.

HIGH-CONTROL EMPLOYEE
BECOMES AGITATED

The *grandiose, high-control employee* becomes intensely agitated.

Alan made a great superintendent. All the foremen under him, the lead men under them, and the workers under the leads pulled together like a star football team. Ray, the owner of J. B. Construction, Inc., had never seen anything like this before; they were ahead of schedule, and under cost.

Part of it, Ray knew, was Alan's vision. He had a way of making the whole crew feel like what they did really mattered. He'd lay out the plan, pat them on the shoulder, tell them to keep it up, even bring a case of beer to the site at the end of the week. He was so active all the time, Ray swore the workers were catching his energy like it was a cold.

Sometimes, Alan did some things that didn't make sense. He'd get a strong but faraway look in his eyes, and if anyone talked to him right then he wouldn't hear them. If he frowned when this look came over him, Alan's face looked like pictures Ray had seen of Jesus on the cross—intense, burning. And sometimes Alan shook his head as if trying to make something fall out, his lips moving the whole time. Ray felt uncomfortable and—he hated to admit this—sometimes even scared when Alan did these things. But Alan was so good, and so productive, that Ray just shrugged it off. Alan had more energy than Ray had ever seen. Maybe that was why he did things that were so . . . different.

"Energy" really was the word for it. Ray wouldn't exactly call Alan upbeat or cheerful. He was more, well, driven. He'd tell a worker, "Good enough, good enough. Now, can you keep it up for the next step?" If someone made a mistake, Alan would say, "Come on, you can do better than that." He always challenged his workers, but in a positive way. It always brought out the best in them.

So Ray was surprised one day to hear Alan complain to Rod about one of the workers in Rod's crew.

"Look, man," Alan said, "you gotta stay on top of this. Don't tell me nothing's any different. The same guy was a lot better yesterday than today. You gotta keep on top of what he's doing. You think God and the devil battle for nothing? You think this guy's soul is all wrapped up when the devil may grab it anytime? We got a battle going on inside, all of us. Your job is to make sure your men are on God's side, okay? You better watch more closely. This is a forever issue. You're talking about souls." Rod looked confused, maybe even afraid. He kept glancing back at Alan as he walked to his crew.

Ray walked up to Alan. "What's going on?" he asked.

Alan shook his head. "It's God and the devil," he said. "When the devil's after the souls of these workers, my leads have to help God more than they do."

Ray said nothing. He felt a cold shiver in his back. Alan had that look in his eyes, but he was smiling.

Ray just nodded and walked off.

Alan is so effective as a superintendent that Ray has trouble acknowledging how unusual some of his behaviors are. And because he's effective, it would be hard for anyone to recognize that Alan had problems.

His "energy" may have meant he suffered from bipolar disorder, or at least had manic episodes, which happened to include productive results. But what looked like energy also may have reflected the bursts of intensity that can come with psychosis. Alan also may have had bipolar disorder *with psychotic episodes*. The point is that whatever the cause, some of his thoughts *and* some of his behaviors are bizarre.

When bizarre ideas or strange connections are put in religious terms, it's hard for most people—especially managers—to reject them. Even the *Diagnostic and Statistical Manual of Mental Disorders (DSM-IV)*, which psychiatrists and psychologists use to identify and label mental conditions, says:

Hallucinations may also be a normal part of religious experience in certain cultural contexts (p. 275); and

> Ideas that may appear delusional in one culture (e.g., sorcery and witchcraft) may be commonly held in another. In some cultures, visual or auditory hallucinations with a religious content may be a normal part of religious experience (e.g., seeing the Virgin Mary or hearing God's voice). (p. 281)

If Alan belonged to a church or other group that believed that performance problems were caused by God and the devil fighting over workers' souls, he could not be diagnosed clinically as psychotic. Interestingly, the hallucinations of psychotics often have religious imagery or symbolism.

Whether or not his strange belief reflects psychosis, as soon as Alan became agitated and obsessive—as reflected in *how* he spoke to his lead man—he became a high-risk employee. Because *what* he said was so strange, the risk was even greater.

When a grandiose and high-control employee becomes agitated and focuses on one thought—especially a strange thought—his behavior is high-risk.

LOSS OF TOUCH WITH REALITY

The *moody employee* loses touch with reality.

> Gary was a pretty good carpenter, but his moods always got in the way. Sometimes he'd be so upbeat you just wanted to hang out with him. But then he'd get very bossy, like he should be in charge or even like he owned the company. Then he'd start chewing everybody out, like they were dirt or something. Then the next thing you knew, he'd be so down in the dumps you felt sorry for him. Sometimes he'd even talk about suicide, and you'd feel so bad that you'd forgive him for how moody he was.
>
> But one afternoon, he did something nobody had seen before. He stood straight up, dropped his hammer and ran from his work, screaming, "No, no! Don't kill me! Don't kill me!"

Everyone stood still and held their breath. A few guys even laughed, but it was a nervous kind of laugh. Was he drunk? On coke? On LSD? Everyone was terrified.

The foreman was the only one who could move. He tackled Gary, pinned him to the ground and yelled for help. As four workers ran toward them, the foreman yelled for someone to call an ambulance.

Later, they found out Gary had "seen" three dead relatives running up to him with guns in their hands.

"It happens now and then," he told his boss and coworkers. "But it doesn't mean anything."

They nodded their heads, as if they agreed.

But no one felt safe working with him again.

What if he thought one of his coworkers was a dead relative with a gun aimed at him? Perceiving his hallucinations as real, he might have done anything to defend himself. Murdering who he *believed* to be a dangerous relative–even though it really would have been a coworker or boss–would have seemed justified to him at the time.

Based on his extreme mood swings, Gary probably suffered from bipolar disorder. His behavior, aside from his moods, was not particularly odd. Yet when the manic stages of his disorder got so extreme that Gary became psychotic, he was as out of touch with reality as any psychotic whose typical behavior is strange.

As Gary's comment indicated, his moods–including his psychotic episodes–occur in cycles. His boss and coworkers have good reason to fear working with him. Gary becomes extremely high-risk as soon as he loses touch with reality and starts hallucinating.

And the switch can be so fast that no one–not even Gary–can see it coming.

CONCENTRATION ON PRESENT IS LOST

An employee *cannot concentrate on the present.*

Toni was quiet and expressionless. Her eyes looked vacant, but she said she could clean up the area and she was willing to work for the three days Bob could promise her. So Bob hired her right there on the spot. Some of his so-called "permanents" were as bad about their attendance as the temporaries from the agency. Maybe Bob would get all three days out of Toni. If so, maybe he'd make her permanent.

For about an hour, Toni wiped the shelves. Then she stood straight up, looked around, and mumbled something. Bob walked over to her.

"Something wrong?" Bob asked.

Toni looked faraway. Her eyes met Bob's for a millisecond and then looked back into the distance. Bob saw tears in Toni's eyes.

"It's the fire," Toni said. Bob looked around, suddenly afraid of arson or sabotage. Toni continued, "As soon as the house burned down. It was the fire."

"What fire?"

Toni tried to look at Bob, but her eyes kept slipping to the distance. "At my house," Toni said. "My father beat us. He was in jail."

Bob felt out of his league. "How about taking a break?" he asked Toni, and nodded toward the gate.

Toni walked to the gate and leaned on it, sobbing. A little later, she left.

Bob shook his head. He still needed someone to help with the cleaning. He still had nearly three days' work to get done.

Then he felt afraid.

What if Toni did show up again?

Because he had just met her, Bob had none of Toni's history with which to compare her current behavior. And because Toni's work was so short term, Bob didn't take the steps managers usually take to get a sense of an employee's history. Bob had no way of knowing it, but Toni was high-risk all along.

She clearly is "elsewhere" in her mind, and cannot concentrate on the work or anything else in the present. She may be schizophrenic or have some other form of psychosis. She may be experiencing the depressed side of bipolar disorder. She may suffer from post-traumatic stress disorder (PTSD) from a history of abuse, and may be experiencing flashbacks. She may be on drugs. Again, as Chapter 11 describes in more detail, your role as manager *excludes* diagnosing. The point is, for *whatever* reason, Toni does not connect with the people, events, or circumstances currently around her.

This lack of connection makes Toni high-risk. Bob has no way of knowing *where* Toni thinks she is, *who* she thinks she is, or *who* she thinks Bob is. Bob cannot predict what Toni might do.

An employee who cannot concentrate on the present is high-risk.

It's always a judgment call. All employees have mannerisms and ways of talking and behaving that are unique to them. It's hard to say exactly when something "unique" becomes *strange*.

As mentioned at the beginning of this chapter, and as discussed in more detail in Chapter 11, *all* high-risk behaviors can come from many different sources, which include histories of abuse as well as the possibility of psychosis. Unusual behavior may come from either–or *any*–of these sources.

Your responsibility as a manager is to focus on the point at which unusual behaviors become high-risk.

You've seen eight categories, each with its own variety of forms, of high-risk behavior. Table 10.1 summarizes the characteristics of high-risk employees. The next chapters describe what you can do about it.

REFERENCES

Diagnostic and Statistical Manual of Mental Disorders (DSM-IV), 1994. American Psychiatric Association, Washington, DC.

Robbins, M. 1993. *Experiences of Schizophrenia*, The Guilford Press, New York.

TABLE 10.1. Characteristic Behaviors of High-Risk Employees

TYPE OF POTENTIALLY VIOLENT EMPLOYEE	CHARACTERISTIC BEHAVIORS OF THIS TYPE OF EMPLOYEE
The Actors	**Act on the basis of their emotions** • Impulsive • Act out feelings, especially anger • Outbursts of rage • Overreact • Exaggerated mood swings
The Fragmentors	**No continuity between actions and results** • Events are like isolated slides • Time is "frozen" at "now" • Repeats the same mistakes • Sees no relationship between actions and consequences
The Me-Firsts	**Focus only on their own needs** • Infant-like awareness only of self • Puts all blame on others • Conveys grandiose, omnipotent self image • Gratification must be immediate
The Wooden Sticks	**Approach Life Inflexibly** • Demands perfection • Rigidly sticks to specific behaviors • Acts in "either-or" ways • Controls people and events
The Mixed-Messengers	**Behave in passive-aggressive ways** • Acts out and "gets even," without acknowledging any problem • Manipulates and hints • Withdraws and, later, gets even • Expects failure and lets it happen
The Escape Artists	**Avoid reality** • Relieves stress through addictive substances and/or behaviors • Distances others • Finds reality too "flat" or boring • Exaggerates credit and minimizes blame • Lies and deceives others

TYPE OF POTENTIALLY VIOLENT EMPLOYEE	CHARACTERISTIC BEHAVIORS OF THIS TYPE OF EMPLOYEE
The Shockers	**Behaviors change suddenly, dramatically, and/or for the worse** • Depression suddenly turns to happiness • Contentment suddenly becomes withdrawal or depression • Good performance suddenly declines • Reliable attendance suddenly becomes erratic • Action is out of character • Action is extreme or inherently dangerous • High-risk employee is fired • Employee is mistreated by spouse/partner
The Strangers	**Remote or withdrawn** • Remote, suspicious employee focuses on one person • Remote, grandiose, high-control employee becomes agitated • Moody employee loses touch with reality • Isolated employee cannot concentrate on the present • Employee is obsessed with plans

Chapter 11

What You *Must*–and *Must Not*–
Do as a Manager When Employees
Behave in High-Risk Ways

Managing high-risk employees requires skills that most managers probably cannot do, have had little or no training in, and until recently, did not even think they would need. Fortunately, no one expects them to manage these employees alone. A healthy combination of teamwork and delegation can solve the dilemma created by high-risk employees.

As a manager, it's important for you to recognize *why* you *absolutely must not* do certain things–and absolutely *must* do others. The following "must nots" and "musts" describe what to do, what not to do, and *why* when an employee acts out high-risk behaviors.

MANAGERS MUST NOT IGNORE
HIGH-RISK BEHAVIOR

It's easy to ignore high-risk behavior if you've gotten used to seeing the employee do it, as in the case of Chuck, in Chapter 9. It's also easy to ignore it if, like most managers, you dislike giving negative feedback to employees. But if you ignore high-risk behavior, it may turn into an immediate danger and a tragedy. In Chapter 9, Jim was more at risk than he realized with his employee Phil. Juan's manager should have taken action instead of covering for Juan's sudden attendance problems. And although Andy documented Betty's performance problems, he ignored Betty's high-risk behaviors.

In addition, *you are vulnerable*—both separately (as the individual most responsible for managing the employee) *and* along with your employer—if you ignore high-risk behavior by an employee who later hurts a coworker. For example:

> The seven other employees in the department had wished for years that Ted would do something about George. George verbally bullied them, butted in when someone else was talking in meetings, screamed obscenities at them when he felt like it, and blamed them for the way he treated them. As his manager, Ted should have started disciplining him years ago. But he never did.
>
> When George showed up one day with a pistol and started shooting randomly around the office, no one was surprised.
>
> But Ted, one of the three survivors, was surprised some time later. He already knew the families of the four murdered employees were suing the firm. But now he found out they also were suing him—for failing to discipline behaviors that, their attorney said, "obviously foreshadowed the murders."
>
> For years, the members of all four families had heard their recently murdered relatives complain about George—and about Ted's failure to do anything about him.

Ted has problems even beyond the emotional and physical effects of the event. Even if he *doesn't* lose the lawsuit, he will have to endure at least two—and possibly more—years of dealing with attorneys, psychologists, legal procedures, and the uncertainty of both the outcome and its effect on him and his family.

If he loses, he also will have financial burdens. Ironically, he was one of the *lucky* ones, because he survived the shooting.

You do not have the choice of ignoring high-risk behaviors. *Instead, you, as a manager, must take action.* The following steps tell you what to do—and what to *avoid* doing—with a high-risk employee.

As a manager, you have no choice. When an employee exhibits high-risk behavior, you must follow these steps.

MANAGERS MUST NOT DIAGNOSE THE "CAUSE" OF A HIGH-RISK BEHAVIOR

This restriction is based on the fact that *all high-risk behaviors can come from many possible causes.* As a manager, you are *un*qualified and *un*able to identify which one has led to an employee's actions. For example, the following list identifies only a *few possible causes* of high-risk behaviors.

• psychosis	• stress	• brain damage
• stroke	• bipolar disorder	• alcohol
• PTSD	• ADD	• anniversary of loss
• brain tumor	• exhaustion	• high fever
• fear	• traumatic situation	• personal problems
• adolescence	• midlife crisis	• menopause
• depression	• religious zeal	• schizophrenia
• grieving	• divorce	• crisis
• hormones	• amnesia	• history of abuse

- medication
- diabetes
- epilepsy
- senility

- puberty
- thyroid problems
- PMS
- poor social skills

- illegal drugs
- personality disorders
- holidays
- other health problems

As tempting as it is–especially as discussed in Chapter 10–diagnosing why an employee exhibits any high-risk behaviors can make the problem worse. You may be misled even when you think the symptom is clear. For example, you may think you smell alcohol on an employee's breath when, in fact, he or she is taking a medication that creates this side effect. You may think an employee is drunk or on drugs when, in fact, he or she is suffering from an epileptic seizure or insulin shock. In Chapter 9, Ty's manager diagnosed the depressed high-risk employee as "feeling better," only to find later that someone had ransacked the manager's home. He had no way of knowing that *revenge* may have caused the sudden recovery. Also in Chapter 9, even the powder and pills Bud's manager discovered do not necessarily mean the manager finally found out the cause of Bud's sudden change in behavior. In Chapter 10, behaviors that clearly make no sense can come from many different sources. Even psychiatrists, neurologists, and psychologists often find it difficult to tell which condition has caused a specific behavior. If these specialists have trouble making a diagnosis, it is clear that managers cannot expect–nor be expected–to do so.

Instead, managers *must* stick to *specific, work-related behaviors*. Instead of diagnosing–"Joe must have had a drink at lunchtime" or "Sue must be having problems at home"–your role as manager requires you to take the following steps.

Identify the Specific Behavior the Employee Exhibits

This has to be an *observable action* the employee is *doing*, and not an opinion, interpretation, nor judgment of your own. One purpose of these clear and specific descriptions is to help manage any anger the high-risk employee may feel. Even if the behavior is subtle—such as a frown or a sigh—you still have to describe it to the employee in terms of what he or she specifically *did* that gave you the idea there was a problem. For example:

"You yelled and swore."

NOT

"You were rude," or "You must have problems at home."

*

"This report has the same math error as your other one."

NOT

"You're terrible in math," or "You must have been daydreaming."

*

"Your eyes look glazed and you've been staring off into space."

NOT

"Are you on drugs?" or "Are you sick?"

*

"You said Jack made this faulty piece, but the log says
it was made on your machine."

NOT

"You're just trying to get Jack in trouble," or "You're hiding
your mistakes."

When you use specific, observable behaviors, you make it easier for the employee to understand *exactly* what he or she did.

The employee can learn from the example or, at least, will be less likely to accuse you of reading into his or her actions, not liking him or her, or picking on him or her. With The Strangers, described in Chapter 10, it is even more crucial to *spell out very literally* what the employees did, didn't do, and should have done, because of how concretely they will interpret what you say.

When talking to any high-risk employees, specific, observable behaviors are relatively objective.

Explain Why That Behavior Is Inappropriate at Work

Once you've identified the specific behavior the employee is doing, explain how the behavior is *potentially dangerous, counterproductive, or in some way inappropriate* at work. As a manager, you must ignore issues that simply involve your personal taste. Focus on behaviors that negatively affect *work or the workplace* and *describe* the problem in those terms. For example:

"I know that safety latch is a nuisance, but if you
keep it tied open like that, you could fall and get killed,"
or "Safety regulations require you to leave the latch alone, and
you've got to follow the regulations."

NOT

"The latch looks silly tied back like that."

*

"When you come in late, someone else has to fill in for you and
then they can't get their own work done."

NOT

"It's not professional to show up late."

*

"If you're staring off into the distance instead of looking at your
machine,
you won't be able to do your work."

NOT

"Quit daydreaming and pay more attention."

*

"When you want your own priorities also to be everyone else's
top priorities, you're forgetting that everyone has other short-
term goals to accomplish."

NOT

"Quit being so self-centered and selfish."

Again, with The Strangers in Chapter 10, you must emphasize
exactly how the problem behavior affects work and the outcome.
The Strangers will interpret your words very literally, and will not
see the relationship between events as easily as you may expect.

With all high-risk employees, when you connect the problem
behavior to the effect it has on work, you again give the employee a chance to learn. At the very least, your description is
clear and objective instead of arbitrary.

Document, in Writing, the Specific High-Risk Behavior, Your Comments, and the Employee's Reaction

Your organization's personnel policies already require you to
document certain events. When you deal with high-risk behaviors, documentation is even more important. You must document, in writing, the *date, time, and place*, what the employee
did, the *effects* of what they did, what *you said and did,* and what
the *employee said and did.* The documentation must include any
additional steps, described below, that you take.

Documentation will help you in several ways. It makes it easier for you to keep *accurate* records–as opposed to a general impression–of an employee's pattern of behaviors. Documentation also provides evidence that the employee exhibited a high-risk behavior and that you, as a manager, took steps to deal with the problem. With The Strangers in Chapter 10, documentation is even more crucial.

When an employee exhibits high-risk behaviors, you, as a manager, must identify the behaviors in *specific, objective, and work-related* terms, documenting the behaviors and your subsequent conversations with the employee.

MANAGERS MUST NOT COUNSEL THE EMPLOYEE

Just as your background and training do *not* include diagnosing, you also are *not* qualified to give employees personal counseling, analysis, or personal advice. The more you care about your employees and the more support and backing you want to give them, the harder it will be for you to tell when you've crossed the line between "helping" as a manager and "counseling." So here's a general guideline: *whenever you use information from your own personal life or something you've read or heard, instead of from your professional training and experience, and whenever the topic goes beyond immediate work issues and into the employee's personal life, you risk crossing the line.*

Regardless of your good intentions, as a manager you easily can make problems *worse* by trying to help an employee deal with personal issues.

Darren put up with Suzanne because he considered himself a good manager. Suzanne had been a good worker for years, and when she fell apart after her husband's death, Darren couldn't blame her for her obvious depression. He couldn't see disciplining her for not dressing properly, sometimes having body odor, or having trouble concentrating on work. He felt sorry for her and wanted to help.

So he invited her to talk with him whenever she felt down. The chats took over every lunchtime, every break, and even led to phone calls in the evening and on weekends. When Suzanne showed up at work one day looking like her old self—nicely dressed, made up, even smiling—Darren felt elated. He commended himself for being there for Suzanne, and went home that evening pleased that her problems were over.

Suzanne went home that evening and jumped out of her sixth-floor apartment window. Darren was right about Suzanne's problems being over. He just didn't know how she would end them.

Nor did he know the reason she felt so relieved at work yesterday was that she finally had her plan in place.

Darren had no way of knowing what *any therapist* would have recognized: suicidal people often feel better after they decide exactly how to do it, and Suzanne's *sudden* improvement in mood meant she was at greater risk than ever.

Because you are *not* qualified—and because an employee may feel so comfortable with you or may respect your authority so much that he or she *thinks* or *feels like* you are qualified—you may in fact *substitute* for the therapist the employee really needs. The employee may listen to you *instead* of getting real help.

Ironically, counseling your employees also may put *you* at risk. Suicide and murder are two sides of the same coin, as in the case of Ed in Chapter 9. Although surprisingly little is known about what goes on inside a person who commits suicide or murder, it is clear that both acts are expressions of despair *and of rage*. In addition to being dangerous to themselves, potential suicides are dangerous to others because the *direction of their rage* is unpredictable. If, at the moment of utmost despair and rage, the target of their feelings is someone else–say, for example, a manager whom they blame for their problems, as Ed in Chapter 9 blamed Ralph–they are more likely to commit murder. If, at the most desperate and rageful moment, the target is themselves, they are more likely to commit suicide, as in the case of Suzanne, above. Because emotions are so volatile at this point, the rage can go either way. It also can go back and forth, leading first to murder and then to suicide. Any therapist knows that he or she–just like Ralph in Chapter 9, and Darren above–also is at risk with a suicidal person. But therapists are more likely than managers to know *when* and *how* to protect themselves.

For all these reasons, you *and* your employees are safer if you stick to work issues and avoid listening to the details of *any* personal issues *any* employees try to share with you, no matter how mild or innocuous the problem may seem or how pleasant and low-key the employee is. Your best reaction is to show compassion and then refer the employee to the Employee Assistance Program (EAP), discussed below. This is especially true if an employee tries to discuss problems involving his or her spouse. If Polly, in Chapter 9, had gone to the EAP, the crisis created by her husband, Walt, could have been avoided. You can be kind and helpful–yet firm–about saying:

- you wish you could help,
- but you're not qualified,
- your focus is on work and not on personal issues, and
- the EAP is the appropriate place to find *real* sources of help.

With The Strangers in Chapter 10, the risk of trying to play the role of counselor is even greater. If The Strangers react to you with suspicion, you are at risk of becoming their target. If they think you are helpful, they are likely to depend on you *and then blame you when their problems only get worse.*

Everyone will be safer if you *avoid* the role of counselor.

Managers Must Refer the Employee to the Employee Assistance Program (EAP) or Another Qualified Referral Source

Find out, *before high-risk behaviors occur*, what referral sources your employer makes available to employees who need personal counseling. If you have an EAP, find out whether it is *internal*—that is, the EAP counselors, who refer employees to outside professionals, are themselves employees of your firm or organization—or *external*, where the counselors, like the therapists to whom they make referrals, work for companies outside your firm or organization. In either case, identify what services the EAP provides, and what steps are involved, under three conditions:

- an employee *voluntarily* chooses to initiate personal therapy, whether or not his or her behavior is high-risk;
- an employee exhibits *high-risk* behaviors and does *not* choose to initiate therapy on his or her own; and
- an employee is *dangerous at the moment.*

Also find out what role the Human Resources (HR) department, the Legal department (or outside attorneys), and Security play under these three conditions. *Find out, as well, what role the EAP, HR, the attorneys, and Security expect you to play.*

If your employer has neither an internal nor external EAP, you must encourage the organization to find an alternative source of *the same services* that EAPs provide. This may mean:

- working with HR, Security, and the attorneys to encourage your employer to gain access to these services;
- working with HR, Security, and the attorneys to identify alternative resources;
- your employer contracting with individual therapists to be "on call";
- your employer offering health insurance that includes the services of mental health professionals;

- HR, or your employer, finding out–from the EAPs in other firms, from companies that provide external EAP services, from professional organizations to which EAP specialists belong, and other sources–what other alternatives are available.

As described below, and in Chapter 13, the *services* provided by EAPs, regardless of what form the source of these services takes, are crucial for both employees and employers.

It also is crucial for HR, Security, and the attorneys to work together in developing and implementing plans.

The Employee Who Voluntarily Seeks Help

Usually, whether internal or external, the EAP *confidentially* refers employees to professional counselors, psychologists, and other mental health professionals. In the circumstances where an employee initiates help, typically he or she goes to the EAP, gets one or more referrals, chooses a therapist, and gets counseling *without his or her manager, anyone in HR, nor anyone else in the organization*, knowing about it.

The High-Risk Employee Who Needs, But Does Not Seek, Help

Under the circumstances where the employee exhibits high-risk behavior, you, as the manager, become involved because you must identify and document the behavior, take steps to get the employee to change it, and find ways to help the employee do so–while communicating in ways, described above, designed to lower any anger the high-risk employee feels. If your employer's personnel policy requires employees to get counseling under certain conditions, find out if those conditions include high-risk behaviors. *If not, do what you can to get your employer to change the personnel policies so that high-risk behaviors do require employees to get professional help. It may help to include HR, Security, and the attorneys in this process.* This requirement makes it easier for you to identify high-risk behaviors, document the threat they present to a safe work environment, *and* get the employee to take seriously—and to *get*—the therapeutic help he or she needs. The requirement can serve as a very important preventive step.

If—or when—your employer's personnel policies include steps for *requiring* a high-risk employee to see the EAP for a referral to a therapist and to see the therapist, the policies also should outline the specific way you, as the manager, can respect confidentiality while monitoring the high-risk employee's attendance in therapy. Usually, this is accomplished in the following ways:

- The *EAP* stays in communication with the *therapist* about whether or not the high-risk employee is attending therapy sessions.
- *You*, as manager, check with the *EAP* about the high-risk employee's *attendance*—which your employer's policies permitted you to require—in therapy. You *never* communicate directly with the therapist, whose identity you will not know and who would maintain confidentiality by refusing to communicate directly with you.
- *You* regularly keep the *EAP* posted about whether or not the employee's high-risk behaviors have stopped. The *EAP* then notifies the *therapist* about the status of the high-risk employee's behavior at work.
- The *therapist* notifies the *EAP* about anything you, as manager, should know—such as the employee's need for medical leave or any increased risk presented by the employee. The *EAP* then notifies *you*, so you can plan for the employee's absence or, in the case of greater risk, take further safety precautions. You will be informed *only* about issues that affect you in your role as manager *and* about any direct

threats the high-risk employee may have made in which you specifically were identified. *Neither the therapist (with whom you do not communicate anyway) nor the EAP will give you any details about the high-risk employee's emotional or psychological issues, or anything about the content of therapy sessions.*

- Your role, as usual, is to monitor the high-risk employee's *work* performance and behavior. Remember that your contact with the EAP relates only to monitoring the required therapy attendance. Also remember that the *only* reason you even know about the therapy is that you had to, and were able to, *require* the high-risk employee to get help.

For everyone's sake–yours, your employees', your customers', the high-risk employees', *and* the employers'–your organization *must* have access to an internal or external EAP, or to another source of the same kind of support. To be prepared to deal with high-risk employees, it is crucial that you know, in advance, what steps your EAP, HR, Security, and the attorneys expect you to take.

As a side issue regarding organization policies, *also do what you can to make sure corporate or agency policies prevent employees' family members from visiting the workplace.* Although the open, family-oriented approach is healthier and more fun–in an *ideal* world–it also makes *everyone* at work vulnerable, just as in the case of Polly's husband, Walt, in Chapter 9.

The Employee Who Is Dangerous Right Now

Under the circumstance where the employee is–or appears to be–immediately dangerous to self and/or others:

- You will need every internal safety and security resource your organization has, including internal EAP counselors. You also may need external police, fire, ambulance, and mental health services.

- In addition to whatever roles HR, the EAP, Security, and the attorneys expect you to play, you must first seek safety for yourself and your employees.
- You then must use any sensible means to contact Security, Safety, the police, the fire department, or whatever resource is appropriate.
- If it is possible–and only if you think it is safe to do so–you can use whatever information you know about the dangerous employee to try to calm him or her down. The purpose is to lower the high-risk employee's anger. For example:

Kyle suddenly stood up at his desk, looking bewildered and waving his hands in the air. He shouted, "I could kill myself and all of you and you still wouldn't care!"

Jesse, the manager, ran toward him and called out, "Kyle, what about your little twin girls? How would they feel if you did that?"

Still looking bewildered, Kyle slumped into his chair, put his arms on his desk, and lay his head on his arms. He started sobbing.

Meanwhile, one of his coworkers had called the police and the EAP counselor. Both were on the way.

Jesse's decision to approach and talk to Kyle–instead of hiding under his own desk–clearly is a judgment call. You know from the previous chapters how ambiguous danger signs can be. You also recognize that Kyle may have been one of The Strangers described in Chapter 10. But usually you know more about your employees than you do about actual strangers–something that might calm them down, and maybe some sense of how likely they are to become physically violent.

In addition, when an employee appears immediately dangerous:

- Notify the employee's spouse, roommate, or someone else whose phone number is likely to be in the employee's personnel records. Do this as soon as possible, even though you are likely to have to wait until after the event.

• Check with the EAP to find out what kind of post-traumatic help can be given to coworkers and others affected by the event.

To be as safe as possible, you are better off dealing with high-risk employees as soon as you recognize the nature of their behavior—*before* they create a crisis or tragedy. Learn, in advance, as much as you can about your EAP or other referral source, your personnel policies, and your own role regarding high-risk employees.

If your employer does not have either an internal or external EAP or other referral source, be proactive about getting one established. If your organization's personnel policies do not make it easy for you to require high-risk employees to get professional help, be proactive about getting your employer to put more "teeth" in the personnel policies. At best, the EAP and stronger policies will prevent crises. At worst, they will help you deal with them.

As you've seen so far, when dealing with a high-risk employee, your first step is to identify the high-risk behavior and explain to the employee how it affects the work or workplace. Your second step is to get the employee to your EAP, or other referral service, so he or she can find a source of—*and get*—professional therapeutic help.

MANAGERS MUST NOT GOSSIP ABOUT THE HIGH-RISK EMPLOYEE NOR HIS OR HER BEHAVIOR

The key here is in the definition of "gossip," and even then, it's another judgment call. Gossip will create problems for you regardless of who the subject is. But if the subject happens to be a high-risk employee, you may become the focus of blame—and the target–of an employee who is unpredictable. As a manager, the following guidelines give examples of what you *cannot* do regarding any high-risk employee or his or her behavior:

- talk to any and all employees within the company or organization;
- talk to vendors, customers, and others outside the company or organization;
- ask the high-risk employee's coworkers for "juicy details" about the high-risk employee's personal life;
- ask for other employees' opinions about the high-risk employee or his or her behavior;
- give your opinion about the high-risk employee or his or her behavior;
- speculate aloud about the reasons for the high-risk behavior;
- ask others to speculate about the reasons for the high-risk behavior;
- talk with other employees about what you think should be done;
- ask other employees what they think should be done;
- say anything that might, in a court of law, be described as "hearsay" or "gossip."

Instead, managers *must* keep information *confidential* and share it only with appropriate professionals. The section above describes how to deal with your EAP or other referral source and with HR. But here, the message is to *contribute nothing to the grapevine.* As a manager, you have more responsibility than other employees to maintain confidentiality about the high-risk employee's personal situation. The following guidelines give you some general ideas of appropriate things to do:

- Keep your direct manager posted about the employee's *high-risk behaviors* and the steps you are taking with the EAP and HR.

- You can answer *questions about safety* asked by coworkers of the high-risk employee, as long as you don't discuss anything else, including your opinions of what the cause is. For example:

> "Steps are being taken to help Rob deal
> with his problems."

> or

> "Rob no longer works here. Steps are being taken
> in case he shows up here."

- You can give the same *safety* information to anyone else who works for the same employer and who therefore may be affected by—or at the mercy of—the high-risk employee.
- You *cannot* discuss anything with the high-risk employee's spouse, family member, or anyone else. Refer *all* these inquiries to the EAP. The EAP counselors and staff will know how to handle them.

The safest thing you can do as a manager is stick to safety-related facts. Avoid all speculation, opinion, analysis, interpretation, diagnosis, and anything else that could sound like gossip or hearsay in court.

Your organization's ability to keep marketing its products and services depends on the safety of everyone who works there. When managing high-risk employees, you *must not ignore* nor *diagnose* their behaviors, *counsel* the employees, or *gossip* about the employees nor the behaviors. With support from your EAP, HR, Legal, Security, and organization policies, you can take appropriate steps to *deal* with the high-risk behaviors, *provide real help* for the high-risk employee, and *maintain a safe work environment* for everyone.

Chapter 12

How Managers Unknowingly
Encourage High-Risk Behaviors

It's tough enough to manage high-risk employees. It's even tougher on your self-image as a manager to realize that, unknowingly, you've encouraged some of their high-risk behaviors. But the problem is organizational, not just individual. Your recognition of how this happens can lead to solutions.

Corporations and agencies neither cause high-risk behaviors nor knowingly encourage them. But decision makers often fail to see the long-term outcomes of organizational policies—outcomes that allow high-risk behaviors to flourish in employees who already have the tendency to enact them. Interestingly, eight informal organizational policies unwittingly support the eight categories of high-risk behaviors.

THE WORKAHOLIC POLICY

This isn't its official title, of course. This policy usually has names like Total Quality Management, Continuous Improvement Policy, or any number of trendy, catchy buzzwords. Ironically, the *purpose* of this policy is legitimate and worthwhile: finding ways to produce and deliver, on the first try, products and services that are high-quality, cost-effective, and satisfactory beyond even the customer's wildest hopes. No one disputes the pressure that global competition and customer-orientation put on corporations and agencies. The pressure is even worse in the context of a shrinking labor force, the sometimes-questioned level of motivation of Generation X, customers and employees diverse in everything from culture to age to gender to lifestyle to market niche, on top of downsizing, reorganizing, and other forms of agonizing. The problem with The Workaholic Policy lies in how it is *implemented*.

The first truth is—and very few managers would admit this publicly—that *everywhere*, there is more work to do than is humanly possible. The second truth is, because of the first, employer organizations *over*work *all* their employees. Sometimes the pressure to overwork comes in subtle forms: the boss arrives at four in the morning and leaves at midnight, you are the only employee who shows up and leaves at the official times instead of working two extra hours at each end of the day, you're responsible for more work than anyone could do in a "mere" forty hours. Sometimes the pressure is more direct: your boss flatly states that he or she expects you to put in eighty or more hours per week, or you work twelve hour shifts and still have to come in for meetings on your days off.

Indirect or direct, the message is clear. You will work ten, twelve, fourteen hours a day, five or six or even seven days a week, and you will spend some of your "time off" either back at work or doing work at home. If your job includes travel, you also face innumerable physical, emotional, and mental stressors, such as time-zone changes, culture shock, language barriers, and often, last-minute notice about the trip itself. When you do all this, it won't be to "get ahead"—it will be to *keep* your job. Perhaps most amazing of all, at a time when good employees are hard to come by, and the laws of supply and demand ordinarily would mean that employers use the royal treatment to entice and keep them, employees today have, in fact, the lowest quality of life since the days of the sweatshops.

This is where workaholism fits in. Because of the current nature of the work environment, those employees with tendencies toward addictive behaviors–The Escape Artists, in Chapter 8–will be the most successful and, therefore, will get the most rewards. To help you understand why this is so, and why it's a problem, here's a brief description of how the addictive process works.

Addiction exists when three things are true:

1. The employee either *does* something that is *inherently* bad for him or her (such as using drugs or alcohol, smoking, or gambling), *or does too much* of something that, in itself, is neutral or even good for him or her (such as eating, exercising, or–you guessed it–*working*);
2. The employee *thinks* and *says* that he or she can quit or cut back anytime, but in reality he or she *can't*; and
3. The substance or activity *replaces personal relationships.* (And you already know, for example, how overworking affects family and other personal relationships.)

Addiction happens when:

1. The employee does *not* use healthy outlets to deal with stress;
2. Instead, the employee tries to *avoid* both the *sources* of stress and the need either to *confront* these sources or make *changes* in order to reduce stress; and
3. The employee finds that a *substance or activity* can help him or her "numb out" or, in the terms of Chapter 8, *temporarily escape* from the stress.

If the employee chooses alcohol or drugs, the addiction eventually will cause *problems* for him or her at work. But if the employee chooses *work* as the addiction, he or she will show up early, leave late, work at home, put all his or her energies into work, do an excellent job–in other words, everything it takes to get *rewarded*. If employers demanded this behavior for a short, clearly specified period of time–for, say, an occasional rush project–this pattern would be insignificant. But when employers clearly expect this behavior *indefinitely*, they are, unknowingly, encouraging addictive behaviors.

If the addictive behavior were limited to workaholism, the corporation or agency might gain in the short term, even though both the employer and the employee would lose in the long term. But because it is an addiction, workaholism presents other risks to the employer organization.

The problems with addictive behaviors include the following:

1. Far from an isolated set of specific actions, addiction is a *pattern* that includes all aspects of an addict's life. Because workaholism is the *only* addiction that, at least in the short term, looks productive and attracts both respect and rewards, managers usually fail to recognize that it *is* an addiction. You saw in Chapter 8 that addiction includes failing to take responsibility, having no control or self-management, being potentially dangerous, and–literally–being out of touch with reality. As an addict, the workaholic fits this description. He or she presents the same risks as any drug addict, alcoholic, gambler, or other addict.
2. Because addiction is a pattern, and because all its forms share the same high-risk behaviors, *poly*addiction–that is, addiction to *numerous* substances or activities–is common. This is even more true today than in previous generations. Workaholics are more likely than other employees to be addicted to drugs, alcohol, or other activities, as well as to work.
3. Most ironic of all, workaholics often use various drugs to help them maintain their demanding schedules. Speed, coke, meth,

and other "uppers" may provide both the immediate energy to get more done *and* the employee's illusion that he or she is doing a wonderful job. Valium, barbiturates, alcohol, sleeping pills, and other "downers" may help the "wired" workaholic relax enough to sleep. While the workaholic is awake, LSD, marijuana, mushrooms, and other hallucinogens may help ward off all the stresses that come with reality.

Ironically, the workaholic is similar to the Escape Artists in Chapter 8: Greg, who uses drugs to relieve his stress; Fred, who distances everyone else; Jerry, whose moods are volatile; Pete, who exaggerates credit and minimizes blame; and Paula, who lies and deceives others, instead of telling the truth. Like any addict–and unlike the image he or she portrays–the workaholic is, at best, irresponsible and, at worst, a high-risk employee who sometimes suffers from self-induced psychosis.

As they currently are implemented, programs aimed at improving quality easily deteriorate into The Workaholic Policy and encourage addiction in employees who have tendencies in this direction. The Workaholic Policy also draws employees who already tend toward addictive behavior. As a result, employers end up with more Escape Artists.

And more risk.

THE MACHO POLICY

This policy fits under the umbrella of corporate culture, as in "changing corporate culture," "paradigm shift in corporate culture," "culture shock," or "we've always done it this way and we don't want to change it." Because, historically, "the way we've always done it" began in an overwhelmingly male environment, it's no surprise that many of the traditional norms regarding work behaviors closely resemble the male stereotype communication style–and that managers of both genders historically have carried out these norms:

- Emphasize *aggressive* behavior
    Whereas *assertive* means weakness
- Self-image as the *"star"*
    Whereas *sharing* means *passivity*
- Goal is to *conquer*
    Whereas *collaboration* means *giving in* or *giving up*
- Wants *control*
    Whereas *inclusion* means *losing power*
- Self-identity hinges on *achievement*
    Whereas a *balanced life* means *being effeminate*
- Communicate by *telling*
    Whereas *listening* means *being dominated*
- Value *self-sufficiency*
    Whereas *needing help* means *being weak*
- *Territorial*
    Whereas *cooperating* means *losing*
- *Competitive*
    Whereas *teamwork* means *losing ground*
- *Dominant*
    Whereas *equality* means *loss of masculinity*
- Value *logic*
    Whereas *having feelings* means *being unprofessional*

These norms discourage openness, honesty, or working together. They also make it impossible to *talk* about feeling frustrated or angry and instead encourage *acting out* these feelings. It's no wonder high-risk behavior—that is, the potential for violence—exists at work. It also is no coincidence that recorded acts of homicide at work began with *male* perpetrators. Although female acts of violence traditionally tended toward *self*-victimization, such as suicide, women who act out violence at work match the profile of the male perpetrator in at least three ways: they tend to be older, long-term employees; they tend to have a fanatic obsession, in this case with their careers; and they have trouble dealing with change. The Macho norms affect women as well as men at work.

As with The Workaholic Policy, no managers carry out The Macho Policy intentionally or knowingly. Overall, the tremendous influx of women in the workforce—including at high levels and in professional fields—has had a moderating effect on the stereotyped male-dominated atmosphere. But history changes its course very slowly, and despite a great deal of hype, the American corporate culture is riddled with images of the characteristics listed above. As a reality check, take a look at the norms, as expressed through the behaviors, in your own organization to assess how different from—or similar to—this list they are.

Ironically, despite its attempts to deny and downplay feelings, The Macho Policy actually *reinforces* acting them out. In Chapter 3, Marc acts on impulse, Larry acts out his anger, Jen has outbursts of rage, Brad overreacts to people, and Roger has exaggerated mood swings. All five typify the "ultimate" macho image. By ignoring emotions—while, at the same time, emphasizing various forms of force and bravado—this policy encourages employees to *act out their problems instead of talking about and solving them.* It increases the likelihood of high-risk behavior on the part of employees who already tend to be macho. The Macho Policy encourages the actors to act out their feelings at work.

The wonder is *not* that we have high-risk behavior at work. The wonder is that there isn't more.

THE SPECIALIST POLICY

Under the banner, "We're State of the Art," this policy says that employees who know a lot about a specific, narrowly defined, high-tech field can get away with not knowing anything else. The more abstract and theoretical their expertise, the more completely this policy will shelter them. They are free of the shackles that restrict everyone else: having to work together with other team members, having to understand how their work fits in with everyone else's, the necessity of dealing with clients' needs, the importance of distinguishing between what they want and what is needed, the importance of selling ideas and getting people to buy into them, the need to resolve conflicts regarding priorities. Without these troublesome restrictions, the specialists have a relatively easy time at work.

They also get only a narrowly focused and tunnel-like vision of the organization's end product or service. Like the Fragmentors in Chapter 4, the specialists see only their own needs, their own viewpoints, their own fulfillments—*without ever seeing or knowing, and therefore without caring about, the impact their behavior has on others*. In Chapter 4, Joe fragments everything, Jean is frozen in time, Al repeats the same mistakes, and Carl sees no connection between actions and consequences. In the same disconnected way, specialists tend to focus on their technology without worrying about how they affect their clients, their coworkers, or other departments. Measuring their effectiveness by how well they perform in the *technical* arena, specialists take no responsibility for problems they may have with people—nor for problems other people have with *them*.

No manager intentionally or knowingly implements The Specialist Policy. But many managers began their own careers as specialists and are too caught up in the policy to realize it even exists. Too close to see it clearly, they do not realize its—or their own—limitations.

Unable, or unwilling, to interpret other people's reactions, specialists' isolation put them in danger of seeing coworkers simply as objects in their work environment, which puts coworkers at risk or, at least, at the mercy of the specialists' moods. Hesitant to communicate their needs or problems to others, specialists tend to act out, rather than talk about, any frustration or anger they feel without considering the effects or consequences. If a specialist has tendencies to become a high-risk employee, The Specialist Policy enhances the opportunities to do so. It places specialists too far away from everyone else.

And the greater the space between them, the higher the risk.

THE ELITIST POLICY

This is a multidiscipline policy, of which The Specialist Policy, above, is a subheading. The Elitist Policy says that certain employees are exempt from the employer organization's rules and official policies. These employees are "elite" not because of their areas of expertise, but because of their informal, unofficial power. Sometimes this power comes from their expertise, as in the case of the specialists above. But more often, it comes from whom they know (either inside or outside the organization), how they look, their personality styles, how long they've worked there, or some combination. Elitists may or may not also have official power, based on their title or position. But even if they do, this policy covers the informal, unofficial side of their power.

Again, managers do not intentionally carry out this policy. They either already are part of the elite, in which case they are too close to see the policy, or they are outsiders who feel intimidated by the elite and are not about to call anyone else on using it. So The Elite Policy stays intact.

Like the Me-Firsts in Chapter 5, the elitists have only themselves to think about at work. In Chapter 5, Brooke has an infantlike awareness only of herself, Darryl blames others for his mistakes, Jim has a grandiose image of himself, and Dave seeks immediate gratification. The Elitist Policy reinforces and encourages these behaviors. It allows elitists to get what they want at work without having to negotiate with others, treat coworkers professionally, compromise with their peers, listen *as well as* speak, rely on others to get part of the work done, motivate employees who report to them, take responsibility for what they do, stay within budget, or meet performance criteria. "Someone" is always there to "protect" them from mundane reality. Elitists are not only *apart* from their coworkers—they're *above* them.

If elitists already have tendencies toward high-risk behavior, The Elitist Policy allows them to think they're "too good" to be restricted by rules, policies, and perhaps even laws. It helps them justify *whatever* they want to do.

And to *whomever* they want to do it.

THE CARVED-IN-STONE POLICY

This policy allows employees to ignore the reality of continual change. It says that if you've been here long enough, you can keep doing what you've always done, instead of having to adjust to new work teams, new methods, new technology, a new workforce, a new approach to clients. Although most managers are unaware of supporting it, this policy works only to the extent that at least a few managers themselves also deny, resist, or fight change. Without these managers to protect them, employees who refuse to accept change would have no choice but to quit or get fired.

In Chapter 6, Ronnie demands perfection in people, Russ rigidly sticks to specific behaviors, Jason has an either-or approach to his behavior, and Bob tries to control people and events. Somewhere in their companies or agencies, some managers have let them get away with their rigidity.

The Carved-in-Stone Policy works only for employees who have been there "long enough." No new employee would get away with refusing to do something different from what he or she learned a week earlier. The length of time required varies with the type of company or agency, but for The Wooden Sticks "qualified" to use it, this policy provides justification for refusing to do anything.

Ironically, it also creates a split between the Wooden Sticks and both long-term and new employees who adapt to ongoing changes. The Wooden Sticks perceive the others as betraying them, putting them down, or foolishly wasting time and money. Those who adapt perceive the Wooden Sticks as holding them back, getting in their way, or even blocking their success. This split can cause and intensify conflicts.

If Wooden Sticks already have any tendencies toward high-risk behavior, The Carved-in-Stone Policy gives them permission to "do whatever it takes" to "bring things back to the way they're supposed to be." It helps them rationalize that they are doing the right thing.

Whatever they do, and however they decide to do it.

THE "HONESTLY, I'M LYING" POLICY

This policy captures the essence of organizational politics, by going at least two directions at once. It says, "Tell me the truth, but because of how powerful I am, make sure the truth is that I'm wonderful." It also says, "This policy demands that no one using it acknowledges the reality of this policy and that, if asked directly, all users will vehemently deny its existence."

Unlike the others, this catch-22 policy usually is well-known to managers who, quick to obey it, publicly deny its existence while privately taking advantage of it. Ironically, the longer a manager has been in his or her position, and the higher the position, the more he or she probably has had to use this particular doubletalk. It is fashionable—and probably also accurate—for managers to show disdain for this policy instead of feigning unawareness of it. If teams ever replace hierarchies, and if collaborative planning ever replaces politics, this policy may die from disuse. But historically, it has been the way of the organizational world. Even then, most managers have seen no connection between this policy and high-risk behaviors.

For employers, The "Honestly, I'm Lying" Policy creates problems. It reinforces–and even rewards–dishonesty and can encourage employees who already have tendencies to be Mixed Messengers in this direction. In Chapter 7, Todd acts out and "gets even" without acknowledging any problems, Bill manipulates others by hinting and being indirect, Michelle withdraws and later "gets even," and Ray expects failure and lets it happen. Their behaviors–and all of the potential for violence–fit right into this policy. When even the managers want flattery instead of the truth, the entire organization is wide open to Mixed Messengers who like to con, manipulate, trick, deceive, and blame others for what they do.

And *do whatever they please.*

THE "GOOD OL' EMPLOYEE" POLICY

This policy says that if an employee is "one of us," he or she can do no wrong. Because of history, it traditionally has meant that if an employee met the mysterious criteria to be "one of the guys," he was a "good ol' boy." Today, either a male employee or a female employee can be one of the guys, or, without gender-bias, a "good ol' employee." The criteria may relate to time, meaning that if the employee has been here long enough, he or she fits in. It may relate to who or how an employee is, meaning that if he or she looks, acts, believes, or in some other way fits the more subtle criteria, he or she is "one of us." The point is that "good ol' employees" are, by definition, innocent or risk-free.

As with The "Honestly, I'm Lying" Policy, most managers are both aware of, and embarrassed to admit their use of, The Good Ol' Employee Policy. To carry out this policy is human. To admit it is to acknowledge that, as a manager, you have taken an impression of an employee, frozen this impression in your mind, and treated it as a stable, unchanging reality, remaining oblivious to changes that may have occurred. This is why The Shockers catch managers off guard. In Chapter 9, Ty becomes happy too suddenly, Ed withdraws too quickly, Phil's work performance suddenly declines, Juan's attendance suddenly becomes erratic, Bud does something out of character, Chuck "always" behaved self-destructively, Betty was "simply" fired, and Polly's husband Walt was "just visiting" her on the job. Their behaviors were easy to miss because it's easy for all managers to think they know their employees—and the employees' families well.

High-risk employees are easy to miss when they blend in and appear to be just like everyone else. Managers have enough to do without closely examining behaviors or subtle changes in one of their "good ol' employees." It's easy for managers to think that an employee they know well is harmless.

It's natural to think this. Familiarity makes you, as a manager, feel comfortable with your employees, their quirks and behaviors, and with any family members you've met.

But it also leaves you vulnerable to The Shockers.

THE "I'M AFRAID TO DO ANYTHING" POLICY

This policy says that if employees clearly act in strange or frightening ways—*even to the point where they do not perform their jobs*—their managers will protect *themselves* by *not* disciplining, *not* documenting, and *not* discussing the behavior or performance problems with these employees. The more unusual and high-risk an employee appears to be, and the more fear the manager feels regarding the employee, the more likely that the manager will move that employee "up and out" or, at least, horizontally. Many employer organizations have high-risk employees who have worked there for twenty or thirty years or more, because managers kept taking turns moving the employees around instead of facing up to, and taking action about, The Strangers' behaviors.

Employees in lower-level jobs, of course—especially those who work directly with The Strangers—know very well how high-risk these employees are *and* how afraid the managers are. In addition to contributing to a high-risk environment, the managers hurt their own credibility. In Chapter 10, none of the managers confronted The Strangers who worked for them.

When new circumstances occur—such as the need to downsize, or the possibility that managers may be held liable regarding the behaviors of high-risk employees—this history of silence will work against them. Because of your predecessors' failure to say anything, you may be the *first* manager to tell a high-risk employee that his behaviors are disruptive or her performance is not up to standard. If no one has corrected The Stranger, and he or she harms or kills someone at work, the well-known facts about his or her behavior may be used against the employer—and the managers—in court.

The "I'm Afraid To Do Anything" Policy increases the risk of dangerous behavior. Your EAP, and all the behaviors described in Chapter 11, will help you overcome your natural fear of confronting The Stranger.

The point is that letting your fear dominate only increases your risk.

IT'S EVEN WORSE
IF YOU COMBINE THESE POLICIES

We've seen eight separate policies that encourage high-risk behavior at work:

- The Workaholic Policy
- The Macho Policy
- The Specialist Policy

- The Elitist Policy
- The Carved-In-Stone Policy
- The "Honestly, I'm Lying" Policy
- The "Good Ol' Employee" Policy
- The "I'm Afraid To Do Anything" Policy

Unintentional as they are, each policy, in its own way, heightens the risk for you, your employer, and your employees. When managers *combine* any of these policies, the risk increases exponentially.

Take a combination of The Macho Policy and The Elitist Policy. Managers who carry out both will, for example:

- act out, rather than talk about, their anger;
- act out their problems, instead of working with the team to find solutions;
- try to control employees, instead of working with them;
- focus only on themselves and their own needs;
- feel isolated from—and "better than"—their employees; and
- assume they can get away with anything.

This combination can lead to these kinds of outcomes:

- A manager gets angry, "for the millionth time," at a "problem employee";
- The manager impulsively fires the employee;
- The manager believes his or her action was justified, because "everyone" knows what a problem this employee has been for the manager, and "everyone" will be glad the manager finally took a stand;
- The manager feels "exempt" from personnel policies, EEO requirements, and other legal issues, because
  - he or she is close friends with the CEO;
  - the employee had one of the lower-paid jobs in the organization; and

- the employee is a high-school dropout, while the manager and most other employees have college degrees;
- The employee feels betrayed, unfairly treated, and wronged;
- The employee's personal life has made him or her extremely sensitive about being rejected or abandoned, and full of rage toward people who think they are "better than everyone"; and
- The employee's sense of betrayal and injustice bring to the surface long-standing resentments he or she has felt toward this particular manager.

A hair-trigger temper easily could turn this explosive combination into a tragedy–regardless of which high-risk profile the employee fits. Each profile would respond dangerously in its own way.

The Actor, behaving primarily on the basis of emotions, would react impulsively to whatever he or she felt at the moment. *Example:* Getting angry and storming off, and returning within minutes, hours, or days–with a weapon.

The Fragmentor, seeing no continuity between actions and results, would fail to consider the consequences of getting even and would react at the moment he or she felt the impact of what happened. *Example:* Harming the manager right then or going away but returning with a weapon weeks, months, or even a year or more later–depending on *when* he or she feels the impact.

The Me-First, focusing only on his or her own needs, would do whatever it took to save face. *Example:* Physically harming the manager; publicly humiliating the manager; sabotaging the manager's office equipment or car; vandalizing the manager's office or house; harming someone close to the manager. This may include stalking the manager.

The Wooden Stick, being inflexible, would see the manager as totally wrong and also would have a sense of self-righteousness that required him or her to get revenge "appropriately." *Exam-*

ple: Harming the manager and/or his or her property or possessions anywhere away from work–such as at the manager's house or in public.

The Mixed-Messenger, being passive-aggressive, would get even secretly and indirectly. *Example:* Appearing to accept being fired, but later sabotaging the manager's car, so that a serious "accident" occurs.

The Escape Artist, avoiding reality, may do nothing for a while but later would seek revenge without admitting it. *Example:* "Forgetting" he or she was fired and showing up at work once in a while, and later, committing burglary and assault or murder in a house that "happened" to be the manager's.

The Shocker, unexpectedly becoming dangerous, would do something dramatic. *Example:* Stalking the manager; threatening the manager over a prolonged period of time; harming the manager in public; harming himself or herself after hurting the manager.

The Stranger, being remote and out-of-touch, would react in ways that are unpredictable but consistent with his or her worldview. *Example:* Walking away, maybe returning to commit arson, and maybe not; harming someone other than the manager who "caused" the manager to fire the employee; harming the manager right then or later; harming himself or herself as well; stalking the manager.

The eight high-risk profiles may react in any number of ways. For you, as a manager, it's important to notice the part over which you can have some influence: in this example, the risky situation came from the combination of The Macho Policy and The Elitist Policy.

Other combinations have similar potential for increased high-risk:

- *The Workaholic Policy and The Macho Policy.* The macho influence could intensify the workaholic orientation–and

the addictive traits that accompany it. The Workaholic
Policy could reinforce The Macho Policy and its destructive
elements.

- *The Workaholic Policy and The Specialist Policy.* The
Workaholic Policy could intensify the self-righteousness of
The Specialist Policy. The Specialist Policy could make The
Workaholic Policy seem more justified.
- *The Workaholic Policy and The Elitist Policy.* The Elitist
Policy could add a more self-righteous quality to The Work-
aholic Policy and its addictive tendencies. The Workaholic
Policy could reinforce The Elitist Policy's sense of being
"above rules."
- *The Workaholic Policy and The Carved-in-Stone Policy.*
The Carved-in-Stone Policy could make The Workaholic
Policy more rigid and inflexible. The Workaholic Policy
could reinforce the status-quo orientation of The Carved-in-
Stone Policy.
- *The Workaholic Policy and The "Honestly, I'm Lying"
Policy.* The "Honestly, I'm Lying" Policy could reinforce
the addictive nature of The Workaholic Policy. The Workaholic Policy could make lying and office politics appear
more justified.
- *The Workaholic Policy and The "Good Ol' Employee"
Policy.* The Workaholic Policy could add addiction to the
"criteria" for being in the "in" group. The "Good Ol' Employee" Policy could increase the likelihood of denying the
addictive elements inherent in The Workaholic Policy.
- *The Workaholic Policy and The "I'm Afraid To Do Anything" Policy.* The "I'm Afraid To Do Anything" Policy
could maintain denial of the addictive qualities included in
The Workaholic Policy. The Workaholic Policy could justify not doing anything about behavior that clearly is high-
risk.

- *The Macho Policy and The Specialist Policy.* Each one could reinforce the other, making the macho managers feel more justified if they also are specialists, and making the specialists feel more justified if they are macho about their isolation.
- *The Macho Policy and The Carved-in-Stone Policy.* The Carved-in-Stone Policy could make The Macho Policy more difficult to change. The Macho Policy could make The Carved-in-Stone more hostile in its implementation.
- *The Specialist Policy and The Elite Policy.* Each could intensify and justify the other. Although both types may look down at each other, they would be unapproachable by anyone else in the organization. Chances for promotion and creativity would be stifled.
- *The Specialist Policy and The Carved-in-Stone Policy.* This combination could reinforce the status quo, inhibit the development of new ideas, and limit the success of the business or agency. It could also intensify feelings of frustration, anger, and helplessness.
- *The Specialist Policy and The "Honestly, I'm Lying" Policy.* Each could reinforce the other's worst traits. Poor work and politics would be institutionalized.
- *The Specialist Policy and The "Good Ol' Employee" Policy.* This combination could prevent recognition of high-risk behaviors among employees who were not only "familiar faces," but who also had technical expertise.
- *The Specialist Policy and The "I'm Afraid To Do Anything" Policy.* The "I'm Afraid To Do Anything" Policy could justify The Specialist Policy's tendencies to avoid recognition of, and confrontation about, high-risk behavior.
- *The Elitist Policy and The "Honestly, I'm Lying" Policy.* Each could reinforce and justify the other. Poor work and dishonesty would be status symbols.

- *The Elitist Policy and The "Good Ol' Employee" Policy.* The "Good Ol' Employee" Policy could reinforce the tendency of The Elitist Policy to ignore high-risk behaviors among other employees, because the followers already see others as "below" them and, therefore, "alike." The Elitist Policy could reinforce the tendency of The "Good Ol' Employee" Policy to ignore small, but telling, differences.
- *The Elitist Policy and The "I'm Afraid To Do Anything" Policy.* By supporting the status quo, The "I'm Afraid To Do Anything" Policy supports The Elitist Policy tendency to keep things as they are.
- *The Carved in-Stone Policy and The "Honestly, I'm Lying" Policy.* Each could reinforce the other. Dishonesty and politics could become the core of the organization's culture.
- *The Carved-in-Stone Policy and The "Good Ol' Employee" Policy.* The "Good Ol' Employee" Policy may reinforce the tendency of The Carved-in-Stone Policy to avoid new information that would "rock the boat." This combination could lead to failure to acknowledge high-risk behaviors at work.
- *The Macho Policy and The "I'm Afraid To Do Anything" Policy.* Each could reinforce the other and intensify the acting out of problems and negative feelings at work.

In the remaining combinations, both policies could reinforce, intensify and justify each other:

- The Carved-in-Stone Policy and The "I'm Afraid To Do Anything" Policy
- The "Honestly, I'm Lying" Policy and The "Good Ol' Employee" Policy
- The "Honestly, I'm Lying" Policy and The "I'm Afraid To Do Anything" Policy
- The "Good Ol' Employee" Policy and The "I'm Afraid To Do Anything" Policy

- The Macho Policy and The "Honestly, I'm Lying" Policy
- The Macho Policy and The" Good Ol' Employee" Policy

The impact increases as three, four, or more policies combine in the workplace. All eight policies–and any combination of them– *unintentionally but effectively* encourage high-risk behavior at work.

No employer organization causes high-risk behavior. No manager intentionally or knowingly acts in ways that invite trouble. These eight policies–and combinations of them–are so familiar that they appear to come with the territory at work.

But, as a manager, you need to look past the immediate outcomes of these long-standing and unacknowledged informal policies. If you miss their long-term implications, you may easily encourage high-risk behaviors in employees who already tend to enact them. You'll encourage behaviors that could hurt individuals, your organization's ability to function, and your organization's standing in the market and community. You'll make your own job even tougher.

And riskier.

Chapter 13

Preventive Steps Managers Can Take to Discourage High-Risk Behaviors: Changing Informal Policies

Taking preventive steps against high-risk behaviors is as proactive as any move you can make. It also may put you so far ahead of your peers' thinking that—like the youngster in *The Emperor's New Clothes* who said the Emperor was naked—you'll need courage to speak your mind and initiate these steps. But corporations, agencies, and managers who make these changes will be at the leading edge of safety, stress reduction, productivity, and marketability.

The first step is to replace the eight informal policies that encourage high-risk behavior, described in the previous chapter, with informal policies that encourage safe and appropriate behavior. This chapter describes effective alternative informal policies, the difficulties you'll face when you try to implement them, and what you can do anyway.

After replacing the eight informal policies, the second step is to provide training to reinforce these new informal policies. The third step involves using job descriptions, performance evaluation processes, and hiring criteria as tools to establish and reinforce appropriate behaviors. The fourth and final step deals with using official organizational policies to require and support safe and appropriate behavior. The second, third, and fourth steps are described in the next chapter.

We begin with the first step, changing informal policies.

FROM THE WORKAHOLIC POLICY
TO THE DO LESS WITH LESS POLICY

The hardest thing about making this change is that you may be the first–and, for a while, the only–manager in your firm or agency to promote The Do *Less* With Less Policy. In an era when most managers look for ways to get *more* work out of *fewer* employees, this new policy may be extremely unpopular. It is, however, more honest, more realistic, more cost-saving, and more lifesaving than The Workaholic Policy. It also will boost productivity by reducing stress. Ironically, you will be saying out loud what all your employees already know but–politically–cannot say.

A report by Northwestern National Life Insurance Co. (1993) describes a study of violence (as well as other issues) at work, and includes the following results:

1. Employees experienced poorer physical health, mental health, *and* productivity, *whether or not* they were victims, following violence or potential violence at work;
2. Thirty-five percent of victims, and 18 percent of nonvictims, suffered from stress-related symptoms, such as anger, depression, and insomnia;
3. Twenty-one percent of victims, and 1 percent of nonvictims, reported decreases in their productivity;
4. Stress at work can both *lead to*, and *result from*, violence at work; and
5. As one of many causes of stress, violence increases employer costs through more medical claims, more disability claims due to stress, decreased productivity, greater turnover, and possible liability risks.

These costs are *in addition to* the risks related to addiction, as described in Chapter 12. Because addiction comes from an employee's failure–for whatever reason–to find healthy ways to deal with stress, increased stress from *any* source means a greater likelihood of addiction among high-risk employees. To the extent that excessive workloads and unreasonable work hours create stress, they contribute to the risk of addiction-related problems. The workloads and hours also will lead, *eventually*, to the increased costs described in the five points above, as well as to greater likelihood of high-risk behaviors. Later in this chapter, you will see various ways you and your employer can help everyone manage stress. For now, while focusing on policy changes, it is important to note that although The Workaholic Policy may look effective in the short term, it will cause numerous losses in the long term.

Hard as it may be to face this fact, the truth is that The Workaholic Policy represents a form of *denial*—just as all addictive behaviors include the denial of the addiction. In The Workaholic Policy, denial hides the reality that *under conditions as they really exist, managers expect more than is humanly possible from their employees*. By focusing only on the short term, and denying the long-term effects, managers act just like The Fragmentors in Chapter 4, focusing only on the present moment with no concern for the future.

The Do *Less* with Less Policy will pay off in both the short term and long term. It means acknowledging that with fewer workers and smaller budgets, you, your employees, your teams, your own manager, and even your customers must decide *what really will get done* and *what may not get done*. Under The Workaholic Policy, priorities determined *when* an employee should do something. Under The Do *Less* with Less Policy, priorities determine *whether* the employee should do it. A task might shift to another employee or team, another task might produce the same outcome that you wanted from the original task, the task may turn out to be unnecessary, or the task may have to be done by the customer instead of your organization—but the bottom line is that at some point, some things *will not get done*. This fact represents the "cold light of day" reality that addicts try so hard to avoid: you can't have–or do–everything.

The Do *Less* with Less Policy will work, *if* you have an effective team of employees, a collaborative and sometimes resource-sharing relationship with your customers, a good sense of what each customer really wants, good work relationships with your peers–and some luck. The time you take, and the energy you spend, to develop these work relationships will come back in the form of *new* ways of doing *new* things more effectively. They also will pay off by reducing the likelihood of high-risk employees enacting addictive behaviors, and becoming Escape Artists who avoid reality.

If you, as a manager, present and implement The Do *Less* with Less Policy, your employees will be surprised, relieved, and eventually less stressed, more accurate, and more productive at the tasks they *do* take on.

After they get over the shock.

FROM THE MACHO POLICY TO THE ADMIT YOU HAVE FEELINGS POLICY

The more your employer organization is dominated by male stereotype values, the harder this policy will be to change. And again, you may be the first manager to replace an old tradition. But the fact remains: feelings will not simply "go away." Your employees have only two choices–to talk about and deal with feelings, *or act them out at work.* If you want to decrease the chances of high-risk behavior on the job, you, as a manager, will have to abandon the macho norms, and establish, role model, and reward a different set of norms. The new norms are neither traditionally "male" nor "female"–they are universal and *professional.* They update the norms described under The Macho Policy in Chapter 12.

- *Assertive* behavior allows everyone to negotiate openly about what he or she wants, thinks, and needs. *Aggressive* behavior guarantees that someone will lose–and it encourages force.
- *Sharing* credit and responsibility is the essence of teamwork. Focusing only on the *stars* leads to resentment, lower creativity, and decreased productivity.
- *Collaboration* means involving everyone in the project, even to the point where customers donate resources and competitors work together toward a common goal. *Conquering*, like aggression, means someone will lose, and again it encourages force.
- *Inclusion* means getting the best work and ideas from everyone. *Control* has the same problems as aggression, starmaking, and conquering.
- *A balanced life* means better health, richer life experience, and at work, increased creativity and productivity. Basing one's identity solely on achievement at work leads to all the problems associated with addiction.
- *Listening* means learning, connecting, gaining insight, and getting new ideas. It also leads to problem solving. Communicating only by *telling* leads to isolation.
- *Needing help* means acknowledging a natural human condition and recognizing that teams make up for what each member lacks. Complete *self-sufficiency* again leads to isolation–and to unrealistic expectations.
- *Cooperating* means making work easier for everyone. *Territorial* behavior prevents employees from being on the same side.
- *Teamwork* means getting everyone's best. *Competitive* behavior, like territoriality, makes everyone in the organization work against each other.
- *Equality* means being honest about the fact that everyone has ideas and creativity to offer. *Dominant* behavior closes the organization to feedback and growth.

• *Having feelings* comes with being human. Feelings must be acknowledged and dealt with, instead of denied and acted out. *Logic alone*, at the expense of feelings, too often becomes a form of denial and, indirectly, *leads to* acting out or high-risk behaviors.

While The Macho Policy encourages employees to act out their feelings–and increases the likelihood that high-risk employees will become violent at work–The Admit You Have Feelings Policy will neutralize the impact emotions have on your workplace. These norms make it clear that feelings such as anger, frustration, and greed *are legitimate but must be dealt with in a realistic and professional way.* They give employees an alternative to denying their feelings or acting them out.

Later in this chapter, you will see how to teach and reinforce The Admit You Have Feelings Policy behaviors. For now, start with your own value system and behavior on the job to see what you have to do to match these new professional norms.

At first, your employees–and probably also your peers–may ignore or resist The Admit You Have Feelings Policy. But the new policy reduces the likelihood that employees with high-risk tendencies will become Actors, acting out instead of dealing with their emotions. Everyone will be able to tell that the new policy is working by how little tension and how much more at ease they feel at work.

And you'll be relieved of having to deal with so much macho, high-risk behavior on the job.

FROM THE SPECIALIST POLICY
TO THE PART OF THE TEAM POLICY

No one denies the value the specialists contribute to your organization. But The Part of the Team Policy aims to lessen their isolation and help them work more effectively with—and relate in less risky ways to—other employees. Any resistance you meet trying to replace The Specialist Policy will likely come from the specialists themselves. The other employees will think it's high time the informal policy changed.

Specialists don't *intentionally* isolate themselves nor see other employees as objects. Instead, their outlook often is so narrowly technical and so ingrained, that how they work with and relate to coworkers *does not even occur to them* as a topic. It is no more an issue to them than how they breathe, and their behaviors can be just as automatic—and, often, just as mechanical. And The Specialist Policy has enabled them to get by without paying any attention to their work relationships.

The Part of the Team Policy requires specialists to deal with the *human*, as well as the technical, side of work. It requires them to find out what their customers want instead of assuming they know, ask what their coworkers need them to do instead of thinking they're doing everything they should, sell their ideas rather than force them on others, listen and discuss instead of giving one-way lectures, and resolve conflicts rather than ignore or deny them. The Part of the Team Policy also requires specialists to *learn about* and *manage* the impact that their behavior, as well as their work, has on customers and other employees. In other words, the new policy requires specialists to see themselves as, and to act like, part of an interdependent team.

Specialists need help developing the skills necessary to carry out teamwork behavior. Specific kinds of help are described in detail below. For now, as their manager, the most important things you can do to start the change to the new policy are:

1. *State that the informal policy has changed.* Specialists need a clear, up front, unambiguous statement that you now require them to be better team members and that you will provide ways (described below) for them to develop the

necessary skills. Acknowledge that The Part of the Team Policy is *new*.

2. *Set the example.* Carry out the behaviors described above, and any others you can think of, to convey the message that you see yourself as part of a larger team. The best the specialists can do is emulate how you treat customers, employees, coworkers . . . and them.

3. *Remember that you are asking specialists to change how they think, as well as how they act.* Even the concept that there are different ways to deal with people is outside the specialist's orientation. You are asking specialists not only to change the way they treat coworkers and customers, but also to see their work relationships in a different way. For this reason, you, as a manager, will have to be both clear and patient. Again, specific ways to help specialists make these transitions are described below.

The Part of the Team Policy will help you bring specialists closer to the rest of the organization. It also will lessen the chance of specialists with high-risk tendencies becoming Fragmentors, seeing no connection between their actions and the consequences.

FROM THE ELITIST POLICY
TO THE EARN IT POLICY

This is a tricky one to change because it deals directly with power. The Earn It Policy says that those with informal power will maintain the proper perspective *as long as the employees who have it also contribute visibly to added value or the bottom line.* As a manager, you may not be able to get anyone else to implement The Earn It Policy unless he or she *has* earned it. And if the managers above you encourage The Elitist Policy, you may be intimidated by an employee whose informal power exceeds your own. But you can, at least, make sure *your own* criteria include issues related to performance and value, as well as to likes and preferences.

While specialists need to learn how to be part of the team, other elitists need to know that organizational rules, policies, performance criteria, and other restrictions—and perhaps even the laws—apply to them. They need to know that despite their informal power—complete with status, special access to people and information, and other perks—they still have to do their jobs and work well with their coworkers and customers.

They also need to hear this fact directly from you and other managers. Potential Me-Firsts need a clear, unambiguous statement to this effect and proof, from your behavior, that you really will hold them to performance criteria and other restrictions.

The Earn It Policy will reduce other employees' resentment of the elitists. Even more important, it will lessen the chance of Me-First elitists with high-risk tendencies focusing exclusively on their own needs and acting—or acting out—as if they're above the rules.

FROM THE CARVED-IN-STONE POLICY TO THE ADAPT TO CHANGE POLICY

The Adapt to Change Policy says employees must be flexible enough to keep learning new ways to deal with both *people* and *technology* at work. This policy is hard to introduce because everyone has some vested interest in "the way it was." But the risk of keeping The Carved-in-Stone Policy has at least as much to do with its *rigidity* as with any particular way things used to be. Rigid thinking can bring out the Wooden Stick righteousness in high-risk employees.

Ironically, when employees resist change, their reaction may not necessarily be to the particular item or situation you, as a manager, are introducing. Instead, they may be reacting to *the fact of change*, regardless of what the specific change is. Just as the specialists above need a different outlook before they can consider how they relate to people, most employees need help seeing their careers and even their lives in a different way before they can become more flexible and adaptable to change. Specific ways to help employees deal with change–and the importance of helping them–are described in detail below. Here, it is important to recognize that the process of change brings with it its own problems and needs for adjustment, in addition to whatever adjustments the specific change requires.

While you take the steps described below, you also will need to be clear and specific about *exactly* the kinds of changes you want employees to make. You can help employees make changes by spelling out your requests in terms of specific, measurable actions and outcomes, similar to the *specific behaviors* described in Chapter 11.

After doing everything you can to describe, encourage, and help with the change process, and while giving recognition to employees doing the most to adapt to change, you also have to set limits on how long you'll tolerate resistance. The longer The Carved-in-Stone Policy backers hang around, the harder it will be for The Adapt to Change Policy to gain credibility and momentum, and the more likely the Wooden Sticks will be to do whatever they think is "the right thing" to do to maintain the status quo.

The more quickly you implement The Adapt to Change Policy, the lower the odds that the Wooden Sticks who tend toward high-risk behaviors will act out their inflexibility at work.

FROM THE "HONESTLY, I'M LYING" POLICY TO THE TELL IT LIKE IT IS POLICY

This one may be even tougher to change than The Elitist Policy. It gets to the core of organizational politics, and perhaps of society itself; egos want to be flattered and also want to believe that the flattery is real. You may be able to change this policy only for yourself.

If managers and employees were willing to hear others' perceptions of the truth, if everyone were trained in ways to tell his or her truth *kindly*, if managers and employees were willing and able to take a problem-solving approach to negative truths, if employees and manager could separate *personal* from *professional* issues—then lying, conning, deceiving, manipulating, tricking, flattering, blaming, and all other passive-aggressive behaviors at work could end.

To be honest, these conditions are hard to create—yet they are necessary to discourage the Mixed-Messengers, high-risk employees who behave passive-aggressively at work. Perhaps you, as a manager, can create these circumstances at least for yourself and those who work for you.

FROM THE "GOOD OL' EMPLOYEE" POLICY TO THE "I'LL SEE THE REAL YOU" POLICY

This policy means paying attention to what your employees *do*, regardless of how you think or feel about them, how well you think you know them, or how familiar their behaviors are. Similar to the way you periodically reflect on employees' work performance, this kind of diligence involves occasionally asking yourself *how employees' behaviors compare to the high-risk descriptions*. Remember, the more of these behaviors you see in an employee, the *more often* you see them in that employee, and the more intense they are, the higher the risk. Remember also that even just a few behaviors occasionally may mean you need to be on guard.

Ironically, those employees you know the best may be easiest to miss. The longer and better you know them, the more likely you are to "explain away" any high-risk behaviors. As a manager, you must keep from being misled by familiarity. At the same time, with new employees, it's easy to miss high-risk behaviors because so much about the individuals is new to you. In both cases, you need to focus on the behaviors and see them for what they are.

Closer and more realistic observation will reduce the frequency of running into Shockers, high-risk employees whose behaviors change suddenly, dramatically, and/or for the worse.

FROM THE "I'M AFRAID TO DO ANYTHING" POLICY TO THE "I'LL SPEAK UP" POLICY

This policy requires you to talk to your employees, speak up when their behavior and/or performance creates problems, and in general, follow all the steps recommended in Chapter 11, as well as the steps described below. Although managers often find this kind of openness and directness difficult with *any* employees, it's easy to see how high-risk employees—especially the Strangers in Chapter 10—can make such encounters frightening.

This policy also means you will need to work closely and regularly with your EAP and with HR, Legal, and Security. The EAP can help you deal with any fear you may have. The EAP can also help you tailor to specific employees the steps described in this book. HR will be helpful in terms of using job descriptions, performance evaluation processes, and even hiring practices, as described in detail below.

As a manager, you *must* address behavior and performance problems at work, for both practical and safety reasons. But you don't have to do it alone.

The first step to discourage high-risk behavior at work is to replace the eight policies that *encourage* high-risk behaviors with the new policies: Do *Less* with Less, Admit You Have Feelings, Part of the Team, Earn It, Adapt to Change, "I'll See the Real You," "I'll Speak Up," and, to the degree you can, Tell

It Like It Is. The short- and long-term implications of *these* policies will discourage high-risk behaviors—and encourage safe and appropriate behaviors—at work.

These new informal policies will enhance employee productivity and your organization's image and ability to meet customer needs. To support these new informal policies, you need the next three steps:

- training that supports the new informal policies;
- criteria for job descriptions, performance appraisals, and hiring practices; and
- official policies that support safe and appropriate behavior.

All three steps are described in the next chapter.

REFERENCE

Northwestern National Life Insurance Co., *Fear and Violence in the Workplace*, 1993.

Chapter 14

Preventive Steps Managers Can Take to Discourage High-Risk Behaviors: Training, Behavioral Criteria, and Other Official Policies

The new *informal* policies, described in the previous chapter, comprise the first preventive step to discourage high-risk behaviors at work. This chapter describes the training needed to support the new informal policies. It also includes the last two steps: behavioral criteria for job descriptions, performance appraisals, and hiring practices; and new official policies.

TRAINING

Whether your employer uses internal trainers, college and university classes, external consultants, programs open to the public, on-site courses, off-site courses, or some combination, the eight new informal policies will be implemented more rapidly and more thoroughly if *everyone* in your organization takes the same courses. Universal attendance will help all employees reinforce each other's behaviors and skills. In addition, even if your company or agency already offers courses in the topics described below, make sure these courses *emphasize the approaches* included in the following descriptions.

Stress Management

Too many stress management classes consist of mood music, ocean sounds, breathing exercises, meditation techniques, and other *relaxation* methods. These skills fit a relaxation course—which may be appropriate (or may not be necessary) for employees after they deal with their stressful situations.

What employees need to help them deal with both their *ongoing* stress and their *immediate* stress are:

- *specific things they can do*, and
- *specific ways they can talk to each other*, that would
- *prevent* stress from occurring in the first place,
- *remove*, through problem solving, the sources of their stress, or
- help them *manage* the internal stress *at the moment* they feel it.

This approach is preventive, cost-effective, and immediately useful to employees.

Remember that everyone becomes more high-risk when under stress. Note that because The Strangers already are higher risk to begin with, they may need more attention from you when they feel stressed. Remember also that addiction comes from employees' failure—for *whatever* reason—to use healthy ways of relieving stress. As a manager, you are *not* responsible for figuring out "why." Your job is to provide ways employees can learn healthy, easily accessible, directly applicable, and straightforward ways to prevent, remove, and manage their stress—*including at the moment a stressful event occurs*. You cannot guarantee that employees will use these skills, but that's *their* choice and responsibility. By offering such classes, you and your employer support all eight new policies and discourage high-risk behaviors in the following ways:

- You make these skills *available* to employees who want to learn them.
- You offer *alternatives* to addiction and other forms of escape, denial through familiarity, macho emotionalism, frag-

menting, complete self-centeredness, rigidity, passive-aggressiveness, shocking changes, and all these categories' forms of high-risk behaviors. Stress management enhances The Do *Less* with Less, Admit You Have Feelings, Part of the Team, Earn It, Adapt to Change, Tell It Like It Is, "I'll See the Real You," and "I'll Speak Up" informal policies. Employees won't be able to say they became violent because they "didn't know what else to do" when they felt angry, frustrated, overworked, or in some other way, stressed.

- You help The Strangers find ways to avoid feeling overwhelmed by external *or internal* stressors. This lowers the potential risk they may present.
- You make it clear that addiction and other high-risk behaviors are *un*acceptable and that you expect employees to deal with their stress more reasonably. This type of course supports your requirements.

The stress management classes should *supplement*, not replace, courses you already offer regarding drug and alcohol problems. They should also include your EAP employees or representatives, either as instructors or as speakers describing the services the EAP offers.

Insist that any stress management course your employer uses takes this practical, applicable approach.

Change and the Grieving Process

Usually thought of strictly in relation to a death, employees in fact go through the grieving process whenever change takes place. This happens because even the most productive changes—say, better jobs or a nicer office location—carry with them some forms of loss, such as the familiarity and comfort of "what was." When employees perceive a change as negative—such as downsizing or reorganization—they experience even greater feelings of loss. Part of the stress commonly associated with change comes from employees' unrecognized and unprocessed grieving.

In addition, current losses can trigger the reemergence of old, unfinished grieving. One way to look at high-risk behavior at work is that current frustrations, problems, and stressors trigger in the employee an *emotional reaction much larger than the present event.* Some of the reaction–for example, some of the anger–comes from the present event, *but a much larger part of the emotion comes from old, unfinished grieving.* You, your other employees, and other coworkers wonder why this employee "overreacted." Even the high-risk employee may think the behavior relates only to the present circumstances when, in fact, it indicates the need to grieve.

Some experts even suggest that psychotic hallucinations–at least under certain conditions–may be replays of unprocessed traumatic memories (Robbins, 1993). It therefore is possible that for The Strangers in Chapter 10, some of their psychotic behaviors relate to unfinished grieving.

All eight informal policies that unintentionally encourage high-risk behavior can be seen as expressing different forms of grieving. The Macho Policy, with its emphasis on aggression and conquest, may reflect the acting out of old, unfinished grieving–particularly of the stage related to anger. The Carved-in-Stone Policy may signify the acting out of frozen, unfinished sorrow. The Workaholic Policy may represent the acting out of denial. Both The Specialist Policy and The Elitist Policy may reflect acting out the numbing, detached stage of shock. The "Honestly, I'm Lying" Policy may represent acting out the back-and-forth process between denial and anger. The "Good Ol' Employee" Policy may signify acting out the need to eulogize who and what was lost. The "I'm Afraid To Do Anything" Policy may represent both denial and the feeling of helplessness.

To support the new, enlightened policies, employees need classes that:

- introduce the *concept* of "the grieving process";
- demonstrate how the grieving process *relates* to change and loss;
- show how *old, unfinished grieving* may be part of their emotional and/or behavioral reaction to an event in the *present*;
- offer alternative ways to *deal with* the numerous emotions related to grieving; and
- include, in the alternatives, *the eight new informal policies* and the *skills* (described below) associated with them.

If you can, have your EAP employees or representatives teach segments of these courses. At least include descriptions of the services offered by the EAP, to normalize this service for employees who need help with the grieving process and to let them know where the help is available.

By offering courses in change and the grieving process, you and your employer validate, teach, and reinforce healthy, accepting ways to deal with emotional pain and adapt to change. You also offer alternatives to high-risk behavior.

Interpersonal Communication

Until relatively recently, work relationships weren't even acknowledged as "interpersonal." The old mechanistic model of management ignored the *people* side of work. The Specialist Policy fine-tunes the art of seeing people as objects—specifically, employees are "machines" to do the work. The Workaholic Policy supports this employee-as-machine approach. While encouraging employees to treat coworkers as objects of their anger or other destructive emotions, The Macho Policy also denies the reality of any human feelings. The Elitist Policy makes other employees "something to be better than." The Carved-in-Stone policy reinforces automaton- or mummy-like behavior. The "Honestly, I'm Lying" Policy is a shrine to two-faced manipulators. The "Good Ol' Employee" Policy emphasizes the image instead of the real person. The "I'm Afraid To Do Anything" Policy, with its refusal to admit there is a problem, "keeps things rolling" in a machine-like way. *All eight informal policies negate the humanness in employees*–which is why they encourage high-risk behavior.

As a manager, you are up against all of these noninterpersonal blocks when you try to implement the eight new informal policies. Yet, similar to the classes in stress management and in the grieving process, classes in interpersonal communication are *essential* if you want to discourage high-risk behavior at work. Your employees need interpersonal communication classes that:

- neutralize the *fear* and *threat* many employees feel when talking one-on-one and in small groups;
- acknowledge that *having options* in how they relate to and communicate with coworkers is new to many employees;
- emphasize *how to speak and behave* in ways that implement the norms and values of *The Admit You Have Feelings Policy*;
- demonstrate the *differences* between *high-risk* and *healthy* communication and behavior at work;
- convey the *benefits* and *payoffs* of, as well as the need for, communicating effectively with everyone on the team;
- identify *specific, observable* skills that comprise clear, kind, accurate, supportive, and useful communication;
- include the *precise* language to use when dealing with The Strangers, who interpret words very literally;
- demonstrate *productive* ways to express *anger, fear, guilt, sorrow*, and other negative feelings, and to deal with *conflict*;
- show employees how to *defend* themselves when verbally attacked;

- include *experiential* exercises, so employees get practice using these skills;
- include ways to communicate in *multicultural* and *cross-cultural* situations; and
- help employees feel *comfortable* in interpersonal situations at work.

The classes on interpersonal communication will establish and reinforce the identity of your employer organization. They also will discourage high-risk behaviors (especially because everyone at work will be able to see how they differ from appropriate behavior) and encourage healthy behavior at work.

To support the eight informal policies, which encourage safe, appropriate behavior, your organization's training must include programs in stress management, change and the grieving process, and interpersonal communication.

As a manager, set an example by being among the first to take all three types of classes, and by carrying out the skills and behaviors they teach. Also, be among the first to send your employees to these classes.

BEHAVIORAL CRITERIA FOR JOB DESCRIPTIONS, PERFORMANCE EVALUATION PROCESSES, AND HIRING PRACTICES

The next step is to work with HR, your peers, and your employees to develop *job descriptions, performance evaluation processes*, and *hiring criteria* that support and reinforce both the new informal policies and the skills developed in the classes on stress management, change and the grieving process, and interpersonal communication. HR can help identify the parameters within which you, your peers, and your employees can develop new criteria, processes, and instruments.

Because employees act on the basis of what actually gets *rewarded*—and ignore what only gets *talked about*—you need instruments and processes that give clout to the norms, values, and behaviors you want to see carried out at work. These norms, values, and behaviors also become the standards that help you, as a manager, define clearly how you want your employees to behave.

Chapter 11 describes the importance of focusing on the specific actions employees carry out. Following the same principle, your job descriptions, performance evaluation processes, and hiring practices all must use, as criteria, *specific, observable, and measurable behaviors, rather than concepts, opinions, judgments, or other general terms*. They should convey, as much like a videotape as possible, what you want employees to *do* and *accomplish* in their jobs.

Job Descriptions

This is the core of the description-evaluation-hiring criteria trio. Yet some firms and agencies do not even *have* job descriptions. In those that do, job descriptions often are inaccurate, incomplete, and/or outdated. Most job descriptions also tend to use words that are *judgments* or *opinions* instead of descriptions of *behaviors*. These situations leave managers vulnerable in several ways:

1. They leave *too much room for interpretation* regarding how employees should work and act. For example, if a job duty is to "work productively," an employee may think this means "produce three units per hour" while you expect *five error-free* units per hour. Both you and the employee would be better off if the job description said, "produce five error-free units per hour," specifying the *behavior*–"produce"–and the *measurable criteria*–"five," "error-free," "per hour"–and omitted the opinion–"productively." Your position is stronger, and your employees are more aware of your expectations, if everything is specific and clear from the beginning.

2. Vague job descriptions make it hard for you to tell *whether the employees understand* your expectations. Because people tend to forget about one-half of what they only hear, written descriptions leave less room for misunderstandings. Written descriptions also make it clear that you are fair and objective, expecting the same results from everyone who has the same job.

3. Vague job descriptions establish *no criteria* for evaluating work performance nor appropriateness of general behavior. The more specific the criteria, the easier for you to be objective, uniform, and fair in evaluating employees' performance. In the example under number 1 above, employees are less likely to argue about who is more "productive" and who "gets off easy" when you spell out "five error-free units per hour."

4. Vague job descriptions *allow high-risk employees to hide* behind the "you never told me" excuse. When you spell out the behaviors you want—in terms of both work results and general behavior in the work area—and when your expectations are in writing, high-risk employees have fewer excuses.

5. Vague job descriptions make it *harder for you to hire* the right employees. When applicants read exactly what kinds of things the job requires them to do, and exactly how they are expected to act in the organization, they can decide whether they are able and willing to comply. These specific criteria also give you standards by which to assess applicants' skills, experience, and behavior.

An effective job description spells out the employee's *output* or *results* and *each duty* in terms of *duty-related behaviors*. For example:

Position: Receptionist
Job duty: Answer the phone

Outcome: The caller either gets the information he or she requested, or leaves a message for the appropriate staff person.

Behaviors: In answering the phone, the receptionist will:
- answer by the second ring;
- say, "Marketing Department, may I help you?"; and
- use a polite and upbeat tone of voice.

The first two behaviors are specific, observable, and measurable. The third behavior uses opinion-loaded words: "polite" and "upbeat." But the purpose is to come as close as possible to describing exactly what the employee should physically *do*. In training a new employee, you could use your own voice to give examples of what you want.

In addition to duty-related behaviors, the job description should include *general* behaviors you expect from each employee. These behaviors should be uniform across all the jobs in your department, and they should support the eight new informal policies that emphasize safe, appropriate behaviors. Use this section to describe three to five *key behaviors* that would enhance your employees' job performance, such as:

General Behaviors for entire team/department:

- *share* relevant information with other team members;
- *initiate* discussions about issues as they arise;
- *ask* your clients what their specific needs are;
- *include* client needs in department planning sessions.

Notice that even these general, non-job-specific behaviors are verbs or action words—specific, measurable, and observable.

Your employees can identify, better than anyone else or any existing job descriptions, what their jobs *really* require them to *do*. Work with your employees to develop accurate and specific job descriptions that will establish, reinforce, and support the eight new informal policies. Empower your employees to continuously update their job descriptions as circumstances change, and to keep you posted about the updates. Remember to include HR and your peers, as well as your employees, in the process.

Performance Evaluation Processes

The best managers give feedback regularly, unofficially, informally, briefly, and succinctly. They include positive feedback—such as praise and thanks—as well as corrective comments, depending on the situation. The best organizations include input from team members and other coworkers in a formal performance review.

So the official performance review should be only *another* time to give ongoing feedback. At the same time, you, your employer, and your employees need this official review process to document what gets said informally. In taking preventive steps to discourage high-risk behavior, you, as a manager, need this process to prove that you've *noticed* problem behaviors, that you've *addressed* them, and *how* you've addressed them. High-risk employees, in particular, often need to "see it in writing" before they believe you mean it.

The performance evaluation process is based on the job description. As the second part of the description-evaluation-hiring criteria trio, the performance evaluation form includes the *duty-related and general behaviors* described in the job description.

Ideally, the evaluation form is a list of all these behaviors, with a rating scale next to each item. For example, using the above job description, the evaluation form would look like this:

	Low	High
Answers by the second ring	1- 2- 3- 4	
Says, "Marketing Department, may I help you?"	1- 2- 3- 4	

	Low	High
Uses a polite and upbeat tone of voice	1- 2- 3- 4	
Shares relevant information with other team members	1- 2- 3- 4	
Initiates discussions about issues as they arise	1- 2- 3- 4	
Asks clients what their specific needs are	1- 2- 3- 4	
Includes client needs in department planning sessions	1- 2- 3- 4	

Notice that the rating scale consists of an *even* number of digits, instead of the more typical *odd* number of digits. The purpose is to avoid the temptation automatically to pick the middle number

1-2-3-4-5

and, instead, to make yourself choose *which side of the middle* most accurately describes the employee's level of performance in each skill and behavior.

Because the *rating* criteria on the evaluation form are identical to the *behavioral criteria* on the job description, the performance evaluation form has *no surprises*. Employees know, all along, exactly what you want them to do, and how you are going to measure it, on the job and in general. You, as a manager, can reward and make suggestions based on each employee's *behavior*–as well as on his or her output or results.

Giving Verbal Feedback

Even with a more accurate evaluation form, based on the job description, and even with a more straightforward rating scale, managers still have trouble talking to employees about performance or behavior problems. The following steps will make it easier for you.

1. *Get others' input.* To the extent that your employer encourages or allows it, find out from the employee's teammates, coworkers, external customers, internal customers, and others how well he or she *produces* the outcomes and *does* the behaviors on his or her job description. You may send the same evaluation form to everyone, asking them to rate the employee's performance and behavior on that form.

More informally, you can ask them in person or over the phone. Find out about Employee A, for example, by:

Asking *customers*:
- "How many times does the phone ring before A answers?"
- "How helpful is A about getting you to the right person when you call?"
- "How does A sound to you when answering the phone?"
- "How much does A ask you about your company's needs?"

Asking *teammates*:
- "How is A about sharing relevant information with you?"
- "How is A about initiating discussion when there are problems?"

Asking other *coworkers*:
- "How much does A include client needs during planning sessions?"

With this input, you will have a broader view of A's performance instead of being limited only to your own perceptions. *Without* specifying who said what, you can use the various viewpoints to come up with more accurate ratings (see number 4, below).

2. *Ask open-ended questions.* "Open-ended" questions invite *descriptions* instead of "yes" or "no" answers. Notice that the questions above ask, for example, *how* helpful A is, instead of *whether* A is helpful. Compare the kinds of answers each question would evoke:

| You: | "*Is* A helpful about getting you to the right person when you call?" |
| Customer: | "Yes." |

*

| You: | "*How* helpful is A about getting you to the right person when you call?" |
| Customer: | "Oh, very. In fact, one time when I called, A even. . . ." |

or

"Well, not very. I know A means well, but usually, I have to call back and . . . ."

You can see that the open-ended questions get you the most information. Again, without specifying what anyone said, you have examples of *results* and *behaviors* you can discuss with the employee (see number 4, below).

3. *Have the employee rate his or her own performance and behavior.* Ask the employee to use the same evaluation form to rate himself or herself *before* the review session. During the session, have the employee describe his or her ratings first. Ask the employee to discuss how he or she chose the score for each behavior. The self-ratings, and the discussion about each one, accomplishes at least four things:

- The employee learns, from his or her own experience, how difficult it is to rate performance and behaviors.
- The employee has a chance to brag, explain, and in other ways give background about why his or her self-rating was so high (or so low).
- This process gives you a chance to learn the details about a situation with which you are only vaguely familiar.
- The employee can ask questions that do not naturally come up during work.

While the employee discusses his or her own self-ratings, your role is to listen. You will benefit in at least six ways:

- You will gain insight about the employee's perspective, which may help you learn how you and the firm look from different angles.
- You may get a different view of a situation you'd only heard about, and you may want to give the employee a higher rating once you know more about it.
- You can get a better sense of the employee's interests, motivators, and future plans and areas in which he or she would like, or could use, more training.
- If the employee sounds unfairly self-critical, you will have a chance to give praise and boost his or her morale.
- You can ask how you can help the employee. He or she may have suggestions or requests that do not naturally come up at work.
- Using the descriptions of the eight categories, and recognizing the limits of generalizations, you can listen for clues about this employee's likelihood of becoming high-risk. Preventive steps, such as classes or EAP referrals, are most effective in the early stages of potential problems.

4. *Tell the employee how you rated his or her performance and behavior, and why.* When you talk about the employee's performance, remember to stick to:

- *what* he or she does, compared to what the job description says;
- *how* he or she does it, compared to the job description; and
- what the *results* or *outcomes* are, compared to the criteria in the job description.

NOT

- your opinion of *him or her*;

- your judgment of *him or her*;
- others' opinions or judgments of *him or her*.

Begin with the employee's self ratings:

You: "You gave yourself a '3' for answering the phone by the second ring. What went into your decision?"

Employee: "Well, I almost always answer the phone by the second ring."

You: "My impression is that the phone often rings as many as eight or nine times before you answer it, and that sometimes the caller gives up before you answer it. Most of the time, it takes four or five rings."

NOT

"You're unreliable about the phone."

NOR

"You do a poor job of answering the phone."

NOR

"You don't care about the phone."

If the employee has an explanation of which you were unaware—such as having to cover too many other receptionists' phones at the same time, or a coworker not covering his or her phone as promised—this is the time to discuss it. It may mean that you need to address an organizational issue affecting your employee. Your rating may (or may not) change, based on new information.

But if the difference in ratings is due to contradictory perceptions of a "2" versus a "3," this is the time to explain the criteria.

Employee: "Well, maybe I do miss it more than I realized. It's just that, well, I'm trying, so I thought a '3' was appropriate."

You: "I appreciate your efforts, but the ratings are based on results. If you never answered it by the second ring, it would have been a '1.' To get a '3,' you'd have to answer it by the second ring almost all the time."

If your information comes mostly from others, you can say so without specifying who said what.

You: "Regarding asking clients about their needs, you rated yourself at '4.' I got input from clients, and based on that, gave you a '2.' There is some perception, at least, that you could be more inquisitive."

Employee: "Which clients said that?"

You: "I think the best way to deal with this issue is to ask each individual client how he or she thinks you are doing. That way, you'll show interest to all of them and find out what level of inquiry each feels comfortable with."

Notice how, in these examples, you:

• stick to *behavior* and avoid personal comments about the employee;
• focus on behavior that is *work-related* and not personal; and
• emphasize others' comments as they relate to *work performance*, instead of sinking into gossip.

If employees take part in writing the job descriptions, they are more likely to understand and buy into the rating scale criteria. When you talk about their performance, each of you has a chance to learn more about the other's expectations and to clarify differences or misunderstandings.

Regarding high-risk or potentially high-risk employees, this nonpersonal, behavioral approach will make it easier for you to:

- *identify* high-risk employees, by assessing their *work behaviors* and their *interactions* with you, other managers, teammates, other coworkers, internal customers, and external customers, and determining whether and/or how many of their current behaviors match those of the eight high-risk profiles;
- *specify* the behaviors you want them to change, the ways in which these behaviors should change, and the resources (training, EAP, etc.) available to help them make these changes;
- *monitor* their progress—or lack thereof—according to your employer's guidelines, with the help of HR and the EAP (or equivalent); and
- have appropriate *documentation* you may need for involving Security, requiring EAP attendance, disciplining, firing, or taking other steps.

By treating even high-risk behaviors as *performance* and *behavior* problems in the work setting, you stay within the limits of your role as manager while still identifying—and taking preventive measures against—potential danger. You also continue to treat all employees as fairly and objectively as possible.

Remember that in addition to the yearly, semi-yearly, or quarterly formal evaluation schedule your employer follows, employees need *informal* feedback almost daily.

Hiring Criteria

When interviewing applicants, you can use the job description and matching evaluation form—in addition to any other organizational criteria–as the bases for discussion. Applicants will know, up front, *exactly* what you expect from them. You will be able to ask what specific behaviors and skills they have *performed,* and what results they have *produced*, that match the requirements of this job. These behavioral criteria contribute to the fairness and uniformity of your hiring practices, and decrease negative surprises.

The behavioral criteria also help you identify high-risk applicants. First, however, you must work with HR, your EAP (or equivalent), and your employer's legal resources to determine *whether* you can refuse to hire an applicant whose "only" limitation is high-risk tendencies. You need the support of these resources because:

- As discussed in Chapter 11, you cannot and must not "diagnose." You need advice from both HR and your employer's legal resources about how to deal with an applicant whom you "sense" could be high-risk.
- As accurately as they identify *current or past* high-risk behavior, the eight high-risk categories–as with even the most sophisticated psychological tests–are not *predictive.* Your "sense" that an applicant "could become" high-risk tells you what to watch for now, and what training or support this individual might need in the future. But under the norm of "innocent until proven guilty," it would *not* serve as evidence in court.

Based on input from HR and your legal resources, you *can* use the behavioral approach to *screen out high-risk behaviors.* To do this:

1. Include, either in each job description or in another document, general behaviors your organization requires of *all* employees. These behaviors can be the safe, appropriate counterpoints to any of the high-risk behaviors. For example, Figure 14.1

shows one behavior from each of the high-risk categories, and a healthy counterpoint.

FIGURE 14.1

High-Risk Behavior You Want to Avoid	Safe, Appropriate Behavior You Want to Include
Acts out anger	Discusses angry feelings and takes a problem-solving approach
Sees no relationship between actions and consequences	Takes responsibility for the consequences of actions
Seeks immediate gratification	Delays, and works toward, gratification
Acts in "either-or" ways	Sees numerous alternatives
Hints about what he or she wants	Openly asks for what he or she wants
Uses addictive substances and/or activities	Uses healthy ways to deal with stress
Suddenly performs poorly	Maintains steady level of performance
Loses contact with reality	Deals with reality

2. Use *only* the safe, appropriate behaviors in your job description or list of employer requirements.
3. *Either:*

• Show this list to the applicant, and ask *open-ended* questions about situations in which he or she did each behavior. For example:

"What's an example of you taking a problem-solving approach when you were angry?"

The applicant's answer will show you:

• how well he or she understood the question and the behavior;

- how comfortable he or she appeared about answering; and
- how realistic, genuine, *and appropriate* the answer appears to be.

Or:

- Keep the list to yourself, and ask *open-ended* questions that will give you data about specific behaviors. For example, instead of asking, "What's an example of your performance level suddenly declining?" you may be better off asking:

  "What are examples of times when your performance was at its *best* and at its *worst*?"

  You can continue with:
  "What kind of time frame was involved when it was so good? When it declined?"

- Notice that some questions *cannot* be asked directly, and that the "answer" must be implied through answers to other questions and/or through your own observations. For example, you cannot get a reasonable answer to:

  "What's an example of you dealing with reality?"

  You are more likely to get an impression from the applicant's other answers and overall demeanor.

The hiring process lets you establish the expectations in advance and, to a great degree, allows applicants to self-select and, hopefully, self-screen. The process also helps you stick to work-related behaviors and treat all applicants uniformly and fairly. Remember to work with HR, the EAP, and your legal resources.

So far, we've seen the second preventive step–training–and the third preventive step–establishing behavioral criteria for the job description-evaluation-hiring process.

The fourth step involves other *official* organizational policies. This may involve changing existing policies or adding new ones.

OTHER OFFICIAL POLICIES

Establish a Proactive–As Well As Reactive–Employee Assistance Program (EAP) or Equivalent

As described in Chapter 11, internal or external Employee Assistance Programs (EAPs)–or their equivalent–are extremely helpful to both employees and employers. All employers should provide access to an EAP (or equivalent).

Even those that have them tend to use EAPs strictly in a *reactive* role, responding to a crisis or giving employees the names of appropriate counselors when asked. This role is appropriate but limited. Your EAP professionals–whether internal employees, external contractors, or another equivalent–also can take a *proactive* role by:

- teaching some of the stress management, interpersonal communication, and change and grieving courses described earlier;
- teaching existing courses–or creating new courses–about substance abuse;
- providing similar training for employees' families;
- identifying steps–tailored to your employer organization– managers and employees can take to prevent high-risk behaviors;
- conducting needs assessments to stay aware of changing needs and problems among employees; and
- offering other educational and preventive services.

In addition, the EAP (or its equivalent) *as a resource* must become visible and familiar to all employees. This awareness will increase the likelihood that employees will get help voluntarily when they need it, and reduce the degree of resistance when an employee is required to get help.

Establish Ongoing Communication Between the EAP (or Its Equivalent), Security, and Your Legal Resources

The EAP (or its equivalent) and Security should share information about high-risk behaviors exhibited at work. The EAP can still maintain confidentiality in the following ways:

1. "Confidentiality" must be defined for employees. Just as therapists, psychologists, and psychiatrists have certain *limits* regarding confidentiality, the EAP professionals must define it in these general terms:

   - It means that the EAP professional *will not discuss any details* about an employee's situation nor exactly what the employee said,
   - *Unless* the employee makes a *specific threat or plan* to harm a specific individual,
   - *Or* the employee indicates that he or she has *a specific threat or plan* to harm *himself or herself.*
   - If any of these exceptions occur, the EAP professional *is required* to notify appropriate persons (such as the police, the threatened individual, the employee's family, etc.).

2. The EAP should have the employee sign a release allowing the EAP to *communicate with Security only about potential risks* that could occur at work. For example, the EAP professional may want to let Security know that "Joe, who is into firearms, has verbally expressed intense anger toward his boss." Note that:

- This is *not* a direct threat. "I am going to shoot my boss" *is*.
- EAP alerts Security to watch for Joe carrying guns, *but the EAP professional does not go into any details about why Joe feels this way, how the situation came about, or any other specifics.*

Remember that the *separate roles* of the EAP and of Security must remain clear. *Only* the EAP (or its equivalent) professionals get involved at all in the employees' personal issues and *only they* refer employees to therapists.

Your internal Legal department, or the external legal resources your organization uses, also should be in the loop. Their main role will be to make sure that *all* the steps taken by managers, HR, the EAP, and Security are within legal bounds.

Keep Nonemployee Family Members and Friends Away from Work Areas

As unfriendly as this may sound, everyone will be safer if employees' family members and friends are restricted to a public visiting area near the entryway. As in the example of Polly and her husband Walt, in Chapter 9, it is impossible for you, as a manager, to keep on top of family relations, friendships, or each individual relative or friend.

A visiting area can be comfortable and attractive. A security guard—or at least an employee responsible for keeping track of visitors—will enhance the likelihood of safety.

Do Background Checks

Working with HR and your attorneys, do everything you can to find out about applicants' work histories (including performance and behavior problems), driving records, convictions, military records, education, and related information. Find out what your options are regarding screening and hiring applicants with high-risk backgrounds.

CONCLUSION

As preventive measures to discourage high-risk behaviors–and encourage appropriate behaviors–at work, the four steps described in this and the previous chapter will put you and your employer on the leading edge, with:

- new, enlightened *informal* policies;
- *training* in stress management, change and the grieving process, and interpersonal communication, to support these new informal policies;
- *behavioral criteria* for job descriptions, performance evaluations, and the hiring process, to establish and reinforce the norms and behaviors of these new policies; and
- *official* organizational policies to support the new norms and behaviors.

By discouraging high-risk behavior–and supporting safe, appropriate behavior–you will attract, and keep, the best employees. Your proactive moves will reduce stress, increase productivity, and enhance creativity.

And your organization's relationships with customers and the community will improve as well.

REFERENCE

Robbins, M., *Experiences of Schizophrenia*, New York: The Guilford Press, 1993, p. 120.

Chapter 15

The Marketing Side: How to Deal with External and Internal Customers If a Crisis Occurs at Work

Despite your taking all these preventive steps—or before you take them—the risk still remains that any of the high-risk behaviors at work could escalate into actual violence. If a violent incident occurs in your organization, you have an additional problem: how to address, and modify, the negative impact the crisis can have both internally and externally.

If a violent act occurs at work, your organization's image and credibility will suffer from the perspective of your external customers:

- consumers;
- board members;
- stockholders;
- vendors and suppliers;
- the media;
- other stakeholders; and
- the public in general.

At the same time, your internal customers—*all* the organization's employees—will be at risk in several areas:

- lower morale;
- lower productivity, in terms of quality and/or quantity;

- less trust among coworkers;
- less trust between employees and managers; and
- less commitment to, and enthusiasm for, the organization.

For managers, in addition to problems directly related to the violent act, a crisis at work also creates problems in *marketing*.

WHAT TO DO IF A CRISIS OCCURS

If an act of violence occurs at work, managers must take the following steps.

Top Management Must Make Public Statements to the Media Immediately

Top management's involvement is necessary because it conveys the seriousness with which your organization views the incident and it adds credibility to your organization's responses. In addition, time literally "is of the essence"–the sooner top management speaks up, the more credible the organization will appear.

Actually, top management will make statements to two audiences: external customers, through the media; and internal customers. Ideally, both external and internal audiences would hear the statements at the same time. But if a choice must be made, the external audience, through the media, should be first, because of the speed with which the media will hear about the incident. This will occur rapidly, even if news personnel *don't* follow the police to your organization–and, very likely, they *will*. If top management notifies the media first, the message to internal customers must come immediately afterward.

In addressing external customers through the media, the organization's goals are to *protect and maintain* the organization's image and credibility. The organization is in a defensive position—although the *style* in which top management addresses external customers must convey professionalism, confidence, and competence rather than defensiveness.

Top management's message to the media should include:

Candid Acknowledgment of the Event

Top management should state that a violent incident, or a crisis, has occurred. Any attempts to minimize or deny the event will hurt your organization's image and credibility. The statement should be clear *but not specifically detailed*. For example:

• *No details should be given until they have been verified.*

"An incident of violence occurred today";

or

"There was a shooting at Company X this morning."

NOT

"An engineer was shot at 9:30 a.m. today while he sat at his desk . . ."

are examples of how the incident can be acknowledged without risking inaccuracies.

• *No names should be given.* Neither the names of the victim(s) nor of the alleged perpetrator(s) should be given. The families of victims should be notified before they hear about the victim in the news—and there always is the risk that the victim is not who you first thought it was. Any mention of the perpetrator's name, *before* the suspect is arrested or in another way *officially* identified, could make the organization liable in a variety of ways.

*Expressions of Concern and Compassion for the Victim(s)
and/or the Families*

Without mentioning names, top management should simply
state an interest in the condition of the victim(s). For example:

"All of us are hoping for the victim's recovery and are
awaiting further news";

or

"All of us are saddened by the death of our coworker and
for the grief experienced by his/her family."

Information About What the Organization Is Doing or Will Do

If you have a plan for marketing under crisis, you can simply
spell out the plan as it applies to this particular situation. If you
don't have such a plan yet, top management's statement should
include:

- *How your organization is working with the authorities.* This
  may involve providing certain information, providing time
  (during work) for appropriate employees to talk to the authorities, and other ways the organization can help authorities determine what happened.
- *Resources your organization will provide for the victim(s) and/
  or the victim(s)' families.* These may include financial help,
  counseling services, or other resources that relate to the needs
  in this specific situation.
- *Resources your organization will provide for employees.* These
  may include counseling, time off, or other services appropriate
  to the situation.
- *Security measures your organization will take.* Because of the
  potential "stigma" associated with violent episodes, custom-

ers, vendors, and others may be afraid to enter your office, store, or plant. It will help to identify extra security measures your organization will take.

- *Preventive measures your organization will take.* Changes in hiring, management styles, or other formal and informal policies should be mentioned, if your organization plans to make them.

Because of the urgency of time, if top management must address external customers through the media before details about your organization's plans are in place, the public statement can give a general outline. For example:

> We plan to work closely with the authorities, to help in whatever ways are possible. We will provide various kinds of support to the victim's family and to our employees. Increased security measures are being explored at this moment, and we also are taking steps to intensify a preventive plan for the future.

Notify the Media About Specific Steps Your Organization Takes

If the media know, for example, about a victim's physical therapy for which the firm is paying, the organization's image may even increase. Be careful, however, that this type of publicity comes across as restrained, rather than self-serving. Your goals in this situation are to *protect and maintain* your organization's image—*not* to build it.

The public statement outlined above, made by top management, will answer external customers' key questions. If top management is pressured to give more details before the information is available or officially verified, it is appropriate to say,

> "We do not yet have that information, but we'll let you know as soon as we do";

or

"It's too soon to give you the specifics, but when they are available, I will notify you."

When top management makes this type of public statement, and when it immediately follows the incident, your organization has a better chance of achieving its goals: protecting and maintaining its image and credibility. Recognize that the public statement is only the beginning, however; the organization must follow through and do what top management said it would do. Following a crisis, your organization's visibility will be greater than ever.

Top Management Must Talk Directly to Employees

Again, the statements must come directly from top management, to enhance the credibility of the message and to lessen the likelihood of rumors. Although all levels below top management should support top management's statements, fewer "deliverers" will mean fewer interpretations–and *mis*interpretations.

In addressing internal customers, top management will cover the same topics as in the statement to external customers through the media. However, when addressing employees, top management will include more specifics about the organization. Top management's goals here are to *reassure and comfort* employees, for the purpose of *protecting and maintaining* employees' morale, productivity, and commitment. Also, as described above, specific actions and resources must follow the message.

Top management's message to employees should include:

Acknowledgment of the Event

Until the facts are clear and officially verified, the same general statements should be made as in the statement to the media–no specifics, no names, nor other details. At the same time, employees must be assured that they will get the details as soon as they are available. Top management can candidly state the intention of preventing rumors. For example:

> All of you know there was a shooting this morning. At this point, we are still waiting to find out the exact identity of the victim and of the perpetrator, and the condition of the victim. As soon as we have that information, we will notify you. However, one of our goals is to eliminate rumors as much as possible. Please avoid jumping to conclusions or making assumptions.

Expressions of Concern and Compassion for the Victim(s) and/or the Families, While Also Showing Stability

Emotion is likely to be strong in the top manager who addresses the employees, especially if he or she knows the victim(s) but even if not. Balance is important—some emotion is appropriate, and may help employees see that the top manager really cares, but a certain amount of self-control also is important. Top management has to show both compassion and stability.

Information About What the Organization Is Doing or Will Do

If current resources or procedures already are in place, you can simply refer to them. If not, include the following:

Resources you will provide for employees. Start with this topic, because it relates most directly to the employees. They may feel fear, worry, grief, and a number of other emotions. Their feelings may get worse, instead of better, over time. If you first address their concerns for themselves, they then will be more likely to listen to the rest of what you say.

The resources you provide for employees should include:

- *Access to counseling.* Regardless of what other medical benefits your organization may offer, it is important to provide incident-related counseling for *any* employee who feels the need for it. It would be appropriate to set a specific limit to the number of sessions and the time frame during which the counseling will be available—for example, ten sessions during the next six months.

  The cost of providing such counseling will be far less than the cost of unfinished grieving, post-traumatic stress, and the resulting low morale, decreased enthusiasm, high turnover, lawsuits, and low productivity.

- *Opportunity to schedule these sessions on-site, during work hours.* Assure employees of the confidentiality of their sessions, and make sure the counselor(s) do the same. By offering the sessions during work hours, you make it easier for employees to get the help they need. You also save productive time by eliminating employees' need for travel.

  If certain employees want counseling off-site, offer this option. Again, the cost is far less than affected employees *not* getting the help they need.

- *Opportunity for education.* Employees experiencing the grieving process and/or post-traumatic stress often benefit from learning more about what they are experiencing. A half-day course, presented by a professional, will replace the counseling process for some employees and enhance it for others.

  Again, the course(s) should be held on-site, during work hours.

None of these resources should be required. They should, however, be offered and widely publicized.

Resources you will provide for the victim(s) and/or the victim(s)' families. By making this your next topic, you will demonstrate your concern for the victim(s) and families, and employees will feel reassured that you would take care of them and their families if they were in the victim(s)' place.

The resources should include:

- counseling sessions, within a specific time frame;
- time-limited pay, even though the victim cannot yet work;
- opportunities for training, if the victim no longer can do his or her job;
- specific financial support for the family in a situation where the victim dies; and
- other support, depending on the organization's policy and the specific situation.

How you will work with the authorities. Let employees know that you will be giving appropriate, relevant information to authorities and that you will provide work time for them to do the same. Assure them of the confidentiality of what they tell authorities.

Security measures you will take. Employees are even more likely than external customers to be afraid to go inside your plant, office, or store. You can reassure them by telling them what additional security measures you will take, or if you do not yet have the details in place, that you are working on these measures.

Preventive measures you will take. While reminding employees that you cannot guarantee anything, tell them of plans—or of the current *development* of plans—to implement the hiring and management methods described in Chapters 13 and 14.

Caution Employees

Caution employees *not* to speak to any media people. Explain that top management, and other designated individuals, are dealing with the media, and that no matter how well-intentioned, employees' comments may create problems for the organization and/or affected individuals.

Keep Employees Posted

Notify them about identities of the victim(s) and perpetrator(s), the condition of the victim(s), progress made by the victim(s) and by the authorities, additional available resources, and everything else they want to know. Your consistency and follow-through will help them see you as a source of stability.

By giving employees this information, and by being open to their input, top management has a better chance of achieving its goals: reassuring and comforting employees, for the purpose of protecting and maintaining employees' morale, productivity, and commitment. Follow-through is crucial, because employees are likely to be more watchful of management than ever.

HOW TO BOOST MORALE, PRODUCTIVITY, AND COMMITMENT AFTER A CRISIS

All these steps increase the *likelihood* that you will protect and maintain employees' morale, productivity, and commitment. To make this likelihood a reality, you will have to:

- implement the steps described throughout this book; and
- *involve* your employees in the process.

Here's how to involve them:

Employees know more than you—or *any* manager—can know about the day-to-day, seemingly "small" ways in which high-risk behavior is encouraged or allowed. They also know more about the seemingly "small" changes that would allow for the identification and prevention of these behaviors. At the same time, employees are likely to be candid *only* if they know that their input will be anonymous.

To get their input while guaranteeing anonymity, hire an external consultant to interview your employees and to get their insights about ways in which the work environment can be made safer. Use this process as a needs-assessment, done periodically, which allows you to learn more about how policies, work structuring and scheduling, teamwork, management styles, procedures, physical facilities, relationships, and other aspects of work can improve. *Act* on employees' suggestions and the consultant's recommendations. *Thank* your employees for their input. *Notify* them about which of their suggestions you're going to implement.

By involving your employees in these ways, you will accomplish several things:

- By giving employees an opportunity for anonymous input, *and* by acting on their input, you will give them a way to get past the feelings of helplessness that usually follow traumatic experiences.
- You will treat your employees as experts.
- You will give them an opportunity to vent to the consultant, after which they are likely to offer useful input.
- You will create an environment in which synergy can take place: after the first or second needs-assessment, followed by your implementation of some of their ideas, employees are likely to be more proactive about high-risk situations and ways to fix them. They also are likely to share their ideas with each other.

By implementing the ideas in this book, and involving your employees in the process, you will provide an atmosphere that will boost morale, intensify employee commitment to your organization, and increase productivity. If you take these steps after a crisis, your timing will help employees recover from the trauma.

If you take these steps *preventively*, you will achieve the same goals—and greatly reduce the risk, and cost, of a crisis.

Chapter 16

Balancing Caution with Compassion

Your role as a manager would be a lot easier if high-risk employees were a different species with clearly identified markings. But, in fact, the high-risk employee is one of *us*, caught up in the tragedies and crises that could befall *anyone*.

The behaviors described in this book are as close as you will come to "markings" that indicate which employees are trapped in high-risk conditions. They do *not* define how an employee inherently "is," but rather at what level of risk he or she might be *at the time*. The markings can be difficult to read.

And the truth is that under the right conditions, *any* of us could become high-risk.

When you identify high-risk behaviors at work, and insist that the employees acting them out get help, you prevent tragedies. Whatever the source of an employee's problems, your steps lower the risk—to other employees, to customers, and to your organization's credibility and image. Ironically, even the employees whom you have to *require* to get help will thank you later. Resistant at first, they tend to realize—after getting the help they need—that you saved *their* lives as well.

If someone recognizes that he or she has the potential to become violent, the appropriate environment can make it easier for this person to get help, voluntarily, without a crisis.

That's why you and your employer should focus on, and take pride in, *preventive* steps, and why it pays to know *in advance* what to do in a crisis and in the early stages of high-risk behaviors.

In addition to being a problem in its own right, high-risk behavior also is a *symptom* of bigger problems here and throughout the world. While we blame everything from humankind's dual (perhaps *multiple*) nature to the amount of violence on television, the bottom line is that the workplace, like the world, is less safe than we thought. Individually, no one is to blame—but collectively, we all are vulnerable to being *both* the victim *and* the perpetrator of high-risk behavior.

So when you, as a manager, run into high-risk behaviors at work, you do everyone a favor by requiring the employee to get help. You and your employer enhance the quality of life for your employees, yourselves, the high-risk employees, your customers, everyone's families—and the society around you.

With the skills described in this book, you are ready to take appropriate *caution* when you face high-risk situations and, at the same time, show *compassion* for the employees caught in them.

The balance between caution and compassion will make your role as a manager a little less tough.

Index